PAINLESS
American
History
2nd Edition

Curt Lader

BARRON'S

All inquiries should be addressed to:
Barron's Educational Series, Inc.
250 Wireless Boulevard
Hauppauge, New York 11788
www.barronseduc.com

ISBN-13: 978-0-7641-4231-4

Library of Congress Catalog Card No. 2009010390

Library of Congress Cataloging-in-Publication Data

Lader, Curt.
    Painless American history / Curt Lader. —2nd ed.
        p.   cm.
    Includes bibliographical references and index.
    ISBN-13: 978-0-7641-4231-4
        1. United States—History—Outlines, syllabi, etc.   2. United
    States—History—Juvenile literature.   3. United States—History—
Study and teaching—Activity programs.   I. Title.

    E178.2.L2   2009
    973—dc22   2009010390

PRINTED IN THE UNITED STATES OF AMERICA
10 9 8 7 6 5 4 3

This book is dedicated to my son Glenn.

Acknowledgments

In describing history, playwright William Inge said, "events in the past may be roughly divided into those which probably never happened and those which do not matter." The events that comprise *Painless American History* have been chosen because they are significant and have made their mark on the course this country has taken. Looking at them and completing the many activities that personalize history, you should come away with an appreciation and understanding of the heritage of the United States. I want to thank the many people who helped and guided me: teachers from Northport-East Northport School District, my wife Phyllis, my sons Craig and Glenn, and my parents.

CONTENTS

INTRODUCTION

To parents and teachers

Painless American History could be viewed by the layperson as a contradiction in terms. How can any history starting with pre-colonial times and ending with a contemporary look at where our country is today be painless?

By using this book, your child or student will be exposed to the National Standards for History, which were developed after four years of intensive work by classroom history teachers, department chairpersons, state social studies specialists, and superintendents of schools. In addition, many historians, civic and public interest groups, parents, and individual citizens took part in this project. The result was the formation of The National Council for History Standards and the publication of a book, *National Standards for History*, published by the National Center for History in the Schools at the University of California in Los Angeles.

Recent presidential administrations from Reagan to George W. Bush have touted the importance of national standards in education. From the creation of the United States Department of Education under President Reagan to the call for reform of the nation's schools by President George W. Bush to the passage of No Child Left Behind under President George W. Bush, there has been a keen interest in raising standards.

Painless American History will make history enjoyable. It incorporates the standards adopted by the national council.

Each chapter contains a Time Line of the major historical events of the time period. The student then has a series of drills that help with an understanding of the content. Some of these activities include mapping an outline, interpreting a Time Line, understanding vocabulary, analyzing eyewitness accounts of events, looking at key historical documents, and reading about some of the key personalities of each era. Interspersed will be lots of historical trivia, key questions to consider, and Internet resources available for further research.

You can play a key role in helping your child or student understand and appreciate American history by talking about what is going on in the world, encouraging the child to read newspapers and ask questions, and by complimenting the child when success is achieved.

To students

American history—YUCCH! That is a typical response from students. Who wants to learn a bunch of boring dates and facts? What good will this stuff do me in the future? Will it help me get a job? What is the connection of history to my life? These are just a few of the questions I've heard at the start of each school year.

Two of my children have completed public school. They have both graduated from college. When they were in the middle school, I was dismayed at the fact that the song that starts with the line "Don't know much about history" applied to many of their friends. Working closely with them, I realized that in order for history to come alive a couple of things had to happen: First, one had to understand what was going on; second, there had to be interesting people, places, and events; third, activities related to each topic had to be exciting.

Painless American History is my answer to those students who don't like to study American history. You are going to take the role of a detective, and accompany Sherlock, who will lead you on a **S**earch **T**hrough **A**merican history **R**esources and make you a STAR! As you travel back through the pages of American history, your job as detective will be to investigate the past, present, and future. You will be able to read eyewitness accounts with imagination. You will make up good questions, read maps, distinguish fact from fiction, and look at historical data.

Each chapter contains a brief summary of some of the key events of the historical era. You will be asked to evaluate what I call "Mind Maps." A good detective knows about dates and each chapter has a continuous Time Line of events. The language of history is essential. Therefore, you will be given key vocabulary for each historical era. Throughout the chapters historical trivia is included. Sherlock will look at some dramatic eyewitness accounts and you will be asked to evaluate them. There will also be activities such as map and document challenges, biographical spotlights, and role-playing activities that will help you understand American History. Internet sites will be referenced in each chapter and the appendix; these sites will enable you to conduct further research.

Important people make significant contributions. By looking at some of the documents that have helped mold our nation, you will develop a better understanding of history.

Icon Descriptions

The following icons will appear in each Chapter of Painless American History. These will help you in your investigative journey through American history!

Eyewitness Account
First person memories of historical events

Chapter Flashback
A short recap of what was covered in the preceding chapter

Mind Map
A diagram that links common themes

Continued

Biography Spotlight
Short biographical sketches of major historical figures

Historical Tidbit
History trivia that increases the reader's understanding of history

Sherlock Challenge
A problem posed by Sherlock, the history detective who will be taking on a journey through American history

Document Challenge
A question posed by Sherlock related to a primary document

Map Challege
A question posed by Sherlock related to a map

Time Line
A chronology of key events that opens each chapter and may appear within the chapter to highlight a series of events

Continued

Matching Madness

A matching quiz found at the end of each chapter based on the contents of the chapter

Definitions

Explanations of important terms and events

Presidential Spotlight

Websites for further reference

Lists of key ideas about a specific topic

Let's begin your journey and investigation . . . .

Web Addresses Change!

Addresses on the Internet are constantly changing. While every attempt has been made to provide you with the most current addresses available, the nature of the Internet makes it virtually impossible to keep abreast of the many changes that seem to occur on a daily basis.

If you should come across a web address that no longer appears to be valid, either because the site no longer exists or because the address has changed, don't panic. Simply do a **key word search** on the subject matter in question. For example, if you are interested in finding out more about the Berlin Wall and the address listed appears to be invalid, do a search for various words related to the Berlin Wall. These are the key words. Key word searches for this topic might include: **Germany, Berlin, wall, communism,** or **Khrushchev.** If an initial key word search provides too many potential sites, you can always narrow the number of choices by doing a second key word search that will limit your original search to only those sites that contain the terms from both your first and second searches.

A number of the passages used in this book, particularly those in the Eyewitness Accounts, can be found at the web sites listed in the Appendix—Internet Resources section in the back of the book.

CHAPTER ONE

Why Study American History?

The stakes are high. It is the challenge that must now be undertaken.
    —Gary B. Nash and Charlotte Crabtree, Co-Directors of the National Standards for History

Time Line (1492–Present)

1492 Columbus "discovers" America
1492–1620 Age of Explorers
1620–1664 European colonies
1664–1763 Competition for colonies
1763–1776 British Empire
1776–1783 War of Independence
1783–1812 Formation of the country
1812–1814 War of 1812
1815–1848 Growth of the nation
1848–1861 Prelude to war

1861–1865 Civil War
1865–1875 Reconstruction
1875–1914 Republic to Empire
1914–1918 World War I
1919–1929 The Roaring Twenties
1930–1939 The Great Depression
1939–1945 World War II
1946–1988 The Cold War
1989–Present Post-Cold War

YOU AND SHERLOCK, THE AMERICAN HISTORY DETECTIVE

Sherlock, your friendly guide to *Painless American History*, has many exciting places to take you. As pointed out in the Introduction, **Sherlock** will make you a **STAR** as you interactively search through American history resources. In doing this, there will be many tasks to accomplish. After you complete them, you will begin to understand that American history can indeed be painless!

    Activities involve "mapping" exercises, using various shapes that contain information related to a topic. Interspersed throughout will be helpful hints, and the outcome of your exploration will be a greater understanding of the heritage of America.

However, before we begin our journey you must obtain the necessary equipment that will allow you to discover the secrets of American history.

THE TOOLS OF THE TRADE

As you progress from historical era to historical era, Sherlock will ask you to use various tools so that you will better understand history. As a result, history will be fun! These tools are descriptive devices that will help you navigate each time period.

For instance, if Sherlock wants you to understand the definition of the **Big Stick Policy,** you will see:

Big Stick Policy—A policy developed by President Theodore Roosevelt that sent a message to Latin America that the United States would take a more active role in Latin American affairs, including the use of military force. The phrase "walk softly, but carry a big stick," was used to describe this policy.

Throughout your journey, you will be challenged to analyze historical events by thinking, understanding, researching, analyzing, and making your own decisions.

First we look at chronological thinking. Before you can start on any historical journey, you must fulfill the requirements by:

- knowing the difference between past, present, and the future
- keeping track of the story
- interpreting and creating Time Lines

Look at the Time Line at the beginning of this chapter. You should see the following historical patterns:

- The involvement in wars is a frequent theme.
- The dates, all arranged chronologically, span the major time periods of American history.
- Knowing this, you can summarize some key issues that relate to the development of our country.
- There are some unique names such as the "Roaring Twenties" and the "Great Depression," which are used to describe historical eras.

Next we have historical comprehension. Here we must look deeper into the meaning of historical events. We do this by:

- identifying and understanding the author or source of a historical document
- understanding the meaning of a historical passage
- coming up with data based on maps, charts, graphs, photographs, and other source materials

For example, look at the following excerpt from the Articles of Confederation:

Title of this Confederacy shall be

"The United States of America".

II.

Each state retains its sovereignty, freedom, and independence, and every power, jurisdiction, and right, which is not by this Confederation expressly delegated to the United States, in Congress assembled.

III.

The said States hereby severally enter into a firm league of friendship with each other, for their common defense, the security of their liberties, and their mutual and general welfare, binding themselves to assist each other, against all force offered to, or attacks made upon them, or any of them, on account of religion, sovereignty, trade, or any other pretense whatever.

DOCUMENT CHALLENGE

What was the tone of the Articles of Confederation? How did the confederation differ from the United States of America that was created after the Constitution was ratified?

Now we turn to historical analysis and interpretation. In this area, Sherlock becomes a critical, analytical thinker. This is done by:

- formulating questions that will help focus on historical analysis
- comparing and contrasting differing ideas
- evaluating historical fiction
- knowing the difference between fact and fiction
- considering different points of view
- explaining causes and effects
- coming up with theories about what has impacted on our past

For example, look at the following list of quotes that were written in 1942 by a Presbyterian minister, William J. H. Boetcker:

1. "You cannot bring about prosperity by discouraging thrift."
2. "You cannot strengthen the weak by weakening the strong."
3. "You cannot help the poor man by destroying the rich."
4. "You cannot further the brotherhood of man by inciting class hatred."
5. "You cannot build character and courage by taking away man's initiative and independence."

Boetcker claimed these quotes were from Abe Lincoln, but historians found just the opposite. The author made them up!

The next area involves historical research. Sherlock uses this skill by:

- formulating historical questions
- getting historical facts
- questioning historical data
- using your knowledge of history to create a story or historical narrative

Painless American History has a companion book that is highly recommended, *Painless Research Projects* by Rebecca S. Elliott and James Elliott, which will "guide you through the process of research and writing . . . and do it *painlessly!*"

One of the best places to do historical research on the Internet is at the Library of Congress at:

> **http://www.loc.gov**
> **Key Word Search: Library of Congress**

In fact, the Library of Congress has a special historical detective who will help guide you through the research process in the following manner:

Start:

1. *You must ask questions (who? what? when? where? why? how?), hunt for clues, talk to witnesses, and visit the scene to search for evidence.*
2. *You must form a hypothesis (I think . . . because . . .) and gather evidence to prove your hypothesis.*
3. *Your evidence must be authentic, firsthand information that you have carefully reviewed to make certain that it is genuine and will prove your hypothesis.*
4. *Brainstorm words. Use the keyword search tool to find evidence. Check your spelling (remember—YOU are the detective, not the computer).*
5. *At a dead end? Use the alphabetical subject listing in each collection to give you some ideas. Scan the list to see what kinds of clues you can find.*
6. *Need help? Ask your school media specialist or teacher. You can also send e-mail to the Reference Librarian.*
7. *Gather evidence. What is your hypothesis (theory)?*
8. *Was your hypothesis complete? Did you find other forms of evidence that caused you to restate your original hypothesis?*

The last area you need to understand before beginning our journey is Historical Issues—Analysis and Decision-Making, where you are:

- identifying problems and dilemmas in the past
- analyzing the different points of view of the people involved
- identifying causes and effects of the problem
- proposing alternative solutions
- identifying the solution you selected
- evaluating the consequences of your decision

This is one of the most exciting areas of historical research.

Let's take a look at the controversial historical decision that was made at the end of World War II to drop the atomic bomb on Japan. An exhibit was scheduled to open at the Smithsonian Institution's Air and Space Museum to mark the Fiftieth Anniversary of the end of World War II. It featured the airplane, the *Enola Gay,* that dropped the first bomb on Hiroshima. This exhibit raised serious questions about how history should represent dropping an atom bomb on Japan. These questions included whether the Japanese point of view should be presented and whether there were other viable options regarding the decision to use the bomb to end the war with Japan. Tom Crouche, the curator of the museum said, "Do you want do an exhibit to make veterans feel good, or do you want an exhibition that will lead our visitors to think about the consequences of the atomic bombing of Japan? Frankly, I don't think we can do both."

HISTORICAL GREAT DEBATE

Do you think the exhibit should have been displayed at the Smithsonian's National Air and Space Museum?

If you follow the format established in the historical issues—analysis and decision making section, you can answer the key question posed: what should be the focus of the exhibit?

Let's summarize Sherlock's tools by looking at this Mind Map outline:

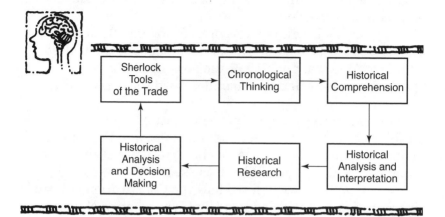

We will be using this Mind Map outline frequently throughout *Painless American History* as a means of introducing or summarizing topics discussed. Your job will be to interpret the diagram by explaining its characteristics.

HISTORY CAN BE FUN

Now that we have the tools of the trade, it is time to proceed on our journey. Sherlock has Searched into Pages from Yesteryear. By taking advantage of your new tools of the trade, you will fulfill the requirements for becoming a detective. These are exciting time periods to explore, people to meet, and events that have shaped the lives of the American people.

In Chapter Two we will begin our trip to the New World as we look at the way the North American continent and its inhabitants existed before the collision with a new European culture. We will follow the journey of Christopher Columbus and the other European explorers.

In Chapter Three we will place the new colonies and settlements under a microscope in what would eventually

become the United States of America. We will explore
political, religious, and social institutions, particularly in the
English colonies. And we will look at the impact of slavery as
a "peculiar institution."

Chapter Four will put you right in the middle of the
American Revolution and the establishment of the United
States of America. Looking at the formation of a new
government, we will begin to understand the workings of
our democracy.

New westward expansion, the impact of the Industrial
Revolution, heightened sectional tensions, and the continued
controversy over slavery are all characteristics of the age of
expansion and reform will be discussed in Chapter Five.

In Chapter Six we will see how the Constitution is tested
as the nation is embroiled in a Civil War where a Northern
Union soldier could meet his Confederate cousin on the
battlefield. The question of slavery is resolved and the nation
emerges wounded but united as Reconstruction begins.

The United States pushing its borders from the East
Coast to the West Coast through the development of the
industrial United States will be discussed in Chapter Seven.
The country is influenced by the rise of corporations, with
"Captains of Industry," massive immigration, the rise of the
American labor movement, and an Indian policy that results
in the containment of Native Americans on reservations.

At the turn of the century, the United States becomes
global. Domestically, a progressive movement of political,
social, and economic reform dominates the agenda. For the
first time in our history we are looking beyond our borders
for raw materials and resources through fighting in the
Spanish-American War. Then the country gets embroiled in
"the war to end all wars," World War I. Chapter Eight will
follow these events and end with the country returning to
normalcy in the decade known as the Roaring Twenties.

Chapter Nine will chronicle the greatest economic crisis
ever to beset the United States, the Great Depression. We
will look at Franklin Delano Roosevelt's New Deal with
its Three "R's"—relief, recovery, and reform—and how it
impacted on our nation. The chapter will conclude with our
entry into World War II, a war fought against two dangerous
aggressors, Germany and Japan.

The postwar United States is characterized by a new kind of war, a cold war, where the major goal is to contain communism. Domestically, the country is transformed socially and economically with the baby boomers, the rise of the birth rate after World War II, and their parents' move to the suburbs. The fight for racial and gender equality reaches a peak, and a new kind of war, the undeclared war, all but paralyzes the United States in Korea and Vietnam. Chapter Ten will look at these events as well as the presidencies of Harry Truman, Dwight Eisenhower, John Kennedy, and Lyndon Johnson.

Chapter Eleven will look at contemporary America from Richard Nixon through Bill Clinton. Domestic and foreign policies, the end of the cold war, and the economic, social, and cultural developments of the United States are evaluated.

Chapter Twelve will look at the new millennium starting with the disputed election of 2000, the tragedy of September 11 and the War on Terror that followed, the wars in Afghanistan and Iraq, and the domestic and foreign policy of George W. Bush. The chapter will also take a peek at the historic 2008 presidential election.

So come, let **Sherlock** lead you through the chronicles of American history.

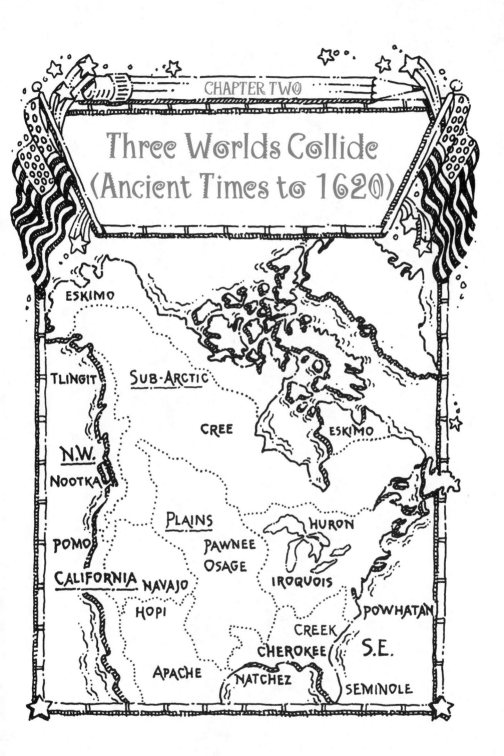

CHAPTER TWO

Three Worlds Collide
(Ancient Times to 1620)

ESKIMO

TLINGIT

SUB-ARCTIC

CREE

ESKIMO

N.W.

NOOTKA

PLAINS

HURON

POMO

PAWNEE

OSAGE

CALIFORNIA

NAVAJO

HOPI

IROQUOIS

POWHATAN

CREEK

CHEROKEE

S.E.

APACHE

NATCHEZ

SEMINOLE

You owe compliance as a duty to the King and we in his name will receive you with love and charity.
   —King Ferdinand's letter to the Taino/Arawak Indians, 1494

Time Line (8000 B.C.–1620)

8000 B.C. Mexican Indians spread culture northward

600 B.C. The Adenans, the first Indian group to build a settlement in what is currently Phoenix, Arizona

First Century A.D. The Hohokum Indians settle in Arizona

1000 A.D. Leif Ericson discovers Newfoundland

1215 The Magna Carta is adopted

1492 Columbus discovers the New World

1497 John Cabot explores Canada

1499 Amerigo Vespucci sights the coast of South America

1507 The term America is used

1513 Ponce de León lands in Florida

1517 Martin Luther launches the Protestant Reformation

1519 Hernando Cortés defeats the Aztec Empire

1519–1522 Fernando Magellan sails around the world

1524 Giovanni da Verrazano discovers the Hudson River

1541 Hernando de Soto discovers the Mississippi River

1565 Saint Augustine, Florida, founded by the Spanish

1587 Sir Walter Raleigh lands on Roanoke Island

1588 England defeats the Spanish Armada

1607 Jamestown founded in Virginia

1609 Henry Hudson explores North America

1619 The Virginia House of Burgesses meets in Jamestown

1619 Twenty Africans are brought to Jamestown for sale, marking the beginning of slavery

1620 *The Mayflower* lands at Cape Cod, Massachusetts

1620 The Mayflower Compact is signed

MOVING FROM
ISOLATION TO INTERACTION

Ancient American cultures

Imagine three separate and distinctive cultures—the
North and South American continents, Western Europe,
and Western Africa. As these societies began to develop,
their influence on each other also began to increase.

Let's begin our story
by looking at the history of
America as it existed before
the first explorers set out on
their grand expeditions. The
first recorded evidence that
the North American continent
became settled occurred
around 30,000 B.C., during the
height of the Ice Age. The first
settlers probably crossed what
is now known as the Bering
Sea to Alaska. Other evidence of early life was found by
archaeologists who discovered artifacts in northern Alaska
and Clovis, New Mexico. Gradually, Indians began to settle
around the river valleys of New Mexico and Arizona.

The first known tribe was called the Adenans. They
began building burial sites and forts around 600 B.C. By the
first century A.D., a dominant Indian culture, the Anasazi,
emerged in what is now Mesa Verde, Colorado. The literal
definition of **Anasazi** is:

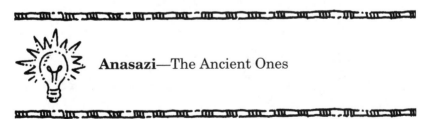

Anasazi—The Ancient Ones

Sherlock wants to take a closer look at the Anasazi culture.

FACTS ABOUT THE ANASAZI

- The Anasazi predated the Pueblo Indians who lived in New Mexico and Arizona. The Anasazi settled in the southwest between A.D. 1 and A.D. 1300. They made pottery, baskets, and tools. Anasazi has been translated by the Navajo as "The Ancient Ones."
- Archaeologists have found ruins of the Anasazi in Mesa Verdi National Park, the Crow Canyon Archaeological Center, and the Mitchell Ruin Group. Archaeologists have discovered cliff dwellings at these locations.
- The Anasazis left the southwest in the late 1200s as a result of a drought.

Other Indian cultures developed after the Anasazi and it is estimated that two to eighteen million Native Americans were in North America at the beginning of European exploration.

The Geography of Ancient America

Let's summarize geographically the dominant Native American cultures that developed in North America prior to European exploration:

- **Arctic**—Located near the North Pole, this area was settled by the Eskimos who lived near the sea and depended upon it for their food. Their housing, igloos, were built to take advantage of the cold environment. Their family units consisted of small groups living in villages and governed by a chief.

- **Subarctic**—This area extends from the middle of Alaska through Canada to the

Atlantic Ocean. The groups in this area include the Tanaina, Cree, Ottawa, and Chippewa. They were hunters and lived in temporary campsites. The head of each band was the most successful hunter.

- **Northwest Coast**—Located along the Pacific Ocean from Alaska to northern California, it is characterized by dense forests and a rainy climate. It is also rich in natural resources. Some of the Indian groups that lived in this area were the Tlingit, Chinook, Nootka, Kwakiutl, and Haida. They lived in villages, fished for survival, and developed into a society of classes that ranged from slaves to chiefs.

- **Great Basin**—An area between the Rocky Mountains and the Sierra Nevada, it covers most of Nevada and Utah. Examples of groups living in this area were the Shoshoni, Ute, and Paiute. These groups were hunters and nomads. They lived in huts and created small family units. Tribal chiefs got their titles as a result of family inheritance.

- **Plateau**—This area covers eastern Washington, Oregon, and the Northwest. The area is like a desert and the rest of it has mountains and valleys, and gets significant amounts of rain. Native Americans in this area were Yakima, Paleuse, and Walla Walla. They fished and hunted for survival and lived in mat-covered houses. Heads of the tribe were selected based on intelligence.

- **California**—The groups living in what is now California included the Chumash, Yokut, Pomo, and Yukis. Because the area was so large, these Native Americans differed in the way they gathered food and in their lifestyle. Generally, they were hunters, lived in villages, and were ruled by chiefs.

- **Southwest**—This is a large area including southern California, Colorado, Arizona, and New Mexico. These groups included the previously described Hohokam, Anasazi, Pueblo, Hopi, and eventually the Apache and Navajo.

- **Plains**—The middle Plains extends from central Canada to Mexico. Plains people are made up of two main groups: villagers (the Wichita, Pawnee, Mandan, Osage, and Omaha), who were farmers and had each village governed by an Indian council, and the nomads, (the Blackfoot, Crow, Cheyenne, Comanche, and the Sioux). They were hunters and more warlike.

- **Eastern Woodlands**—This area stretches from southern Canada to Tennessee and from the Mississippi to the Atlantic Ocean. This area was home to such groups as the Fox, Miami, Shawnee, Sac, Huron, and Winnebago. Other groups included the Iroquois, Pequot, Mohegan, Narrangansett, Delaware, and Powhatan. These tribes had many skills. They usually lived in villages and built traditional wigwams.

- **Southeast**—This geographic area extends from Texas to the Atlantic Ocean and from Tennessee to Florida. Native Americans in this area include the Creek, Chickasaw, Choctaw, Cherokee, Natchez, and Seminole. They were hunters and they set up villages. Some tribes had councils; others were divided into classes.

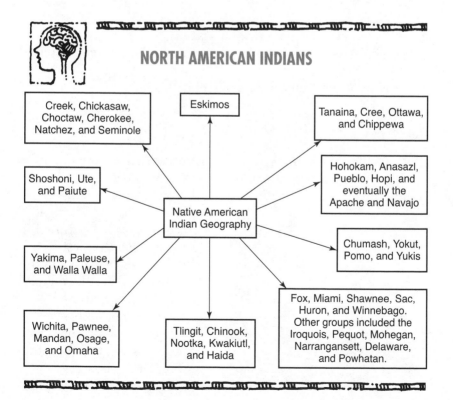

NORTH AMERICAN INDIANS

| Creek, Chickasaw, Choctaw, Cherokee, Natchez, and Seminole |
| Eskimos |
| Tanaina, Cree, Ottawa, and Chippewa |
| Shoshoni, Ute, and Paiute |
| Hohokam, Anasazl, Pueblo, Hopi, and eventually the Apache and Navajo |
| Native American Indian Geography |
| Chumash, Yokut, Pomo, and Yukis |
| Yakima, Paleuse, and Walla Walla |
| Wichita, Pawnee, Mandan, Osage, and Omaha |
| Tlingit, Chinook, Nootka, Kwakiutl, and Haida |
| Fox, Miami, Shawnee, Sac, Huron, and Winnebago. Other groups included the Iroquois, Pequot, Mohegan, Narrangansett, Delaware, and Powhatan. |

Look at the Mind Map depiction of the location of the North American Indians and label each of the areas where Native American groups settled. Then look at the names of the Native American groups. Can you identify any cities that were named after them?

If you take a look at the Mind Map and an actual map of North America, you will notice that the individual Native American groups are placed on the map in a similar manner geographically as an actual map. For instance, the Eskimos are placed on top similar to their real location near the North Pole. The Chumash, Yokut, Pomo, and Yukis represent California, and the Fox, Miami, Shawnee, and the rest of that group represent Indians along the East Coast. As far as the relationship of Indian groups to names of geographic areas, the following groups fit that category:

- Yakima and Walla Walla are cities in Washington.
- Ottawa is a city in Canada.
- Omaha is a city in Nebraska.
- Miami is a city in Florida.
- Narrangansett is a city in Rhode Island.
- Delaware is the name of a state.
- Winnebago has been used as a name for a recreational vehicle.
- Natchez is a city in Mississippi.

Leif Ericson and the Vikings

Before we can get to the first European explorers, we must look at what many historians believe to be the group that should be given the credit for first discovering America—Leif

Ericson and the Vikings. According to legend, Leif Ericson was the first European to actually land in the New World. His discovery opened the way for other Viking voyages. Perhaps, because of rough seas, the climate, or injuries, Viking voyages were limited and

overshadowed by European exploration. It was not until 1963, when the ruins of some Viking houses were discovered at L'Anse-aux-Meadows in Newfoundland, that their voyages were confirmed.

BIOGRAPHY SPOTLIGHT

The interesting thing about Leif Ericson's biography is the extent to which he was influenced by others. Throughout his life, he developed his character from Thryker, the man he moved in with when he was eight years old, and Eric the Red, Leif's father.

Leif was also influenced throughout the rest of his life by the experiences he faced on the journeys that took him to Greenland, Iceland, and eventually, Newfoundland. Each trip taught him leadership skills. His relationship with King Olaf was close and eventually influenced Leif to turn to Christianity.

The final journey to L'Anse-aux-Meadows, in Newfoundland, signified the discovery of the Western world years before Columbus made his maiden voyage.

EARLY EUROPEAN EXPLORATION AND COLONIZATION

Trade and the desire for new routes became the key motivation for Spain, Portugal, and Great Britain to begin exploration. What they, of course, did not realize was that instead of finding a faster way to Asia, they began the quest for colonization of a new world.

Look at the Time Line at the beginning of this chapter. Make a list of the explorers and the land they discovered. What conclusions can you reach regarding the competition among the European nations? Was there any indication of Native American reaction to these explorers?

A list of explorers appears on pages 25–26 and is organized by the country from which they each began their exploration. Looking at the list and at the Time Line, you will notice that Spain, England, and France emerge as the three main countries that commissioned explorers. You will also notice that Captain John Smith was captured by Chief Powhatan and was eventually rescued by Pocahontas.

The Magna Carta

A key event in Great Britain that later had a significant impact on the democratic values in the United States was the signing of the **Magna Carta** in 1215.

The Magna Carta—Also known as the Great Charter; it guaranteed rights such as trial by jury, reduced the rights of the English monarch, and resulted in the creation of the Parliament.

DOCUMENT CHALLENGE

Look at an excerpt from the Magna Carta. Explain what freedoms are guaranteed. Then look at the Bill of Rights and explain which freedoms listed in the Magna Carta also appear in the Bill of Rights.

In the future no official shall place a man on trial upon his own supported statement, without producing credible witnesses to the truth of it.

The entire document can be viewed online by doing a search for "Magna Carta."

The Magna Carta is one of the most important documents to signal the acceptance of democratic values. The portion that was quoted above is similar to our own Bill of Rights in the following way:

- The Bill of Rights requires that a witness be used to prove there is a crime.
- It also requires a trial by jury.
- It has a provision that calls for a fair and speedy trial.

Now, let's look closely at the start of the exploration of the New World by examining the voyages of Christopher Columbus.

Columbus's Voyages

First Voyage, 1492–1493
San Salvador,
The Bahamas
Cuba
Hispaniola

Second Voyage, 1493–1494
Dominica
Hispaniola
Guadeloupe
Antigua
Puerto Rico
Cuba
Jamaica

Third Expedition, 1498–1500
St. Vincent
Grenada Trinidad
Margarita
Venezuela

Fourth Expedition, 1502–1504
St. Lucia
Martinique
Honduras
Nicaragua
Costa Rica
Panama

Find these places on a map.

DOCUMENT CHALLENGE

Look at an illustration of Christopher Columbus's Coat of Arms that is part of the Library of Congress exhibit, 1492, an Ongoing Voyage:

What can you determine about Christopher Columbus from this coat of arms?

HISTORICAL TIDBIT

Did you know that Columbus maintained two logs, an official one that he kept private and a made-up one that provided false information to the crew in order to keep them calm about the long journey? It turned out that the false log was more accurate.

After Columbus landed in the Caribbean, the New World became a mecca for exploration.

Let's take a look at the significant discoveries by country and evaluate their importance to the development of early settlements.

Spanish conquests

- In 1499 the Italian explorer **Amerigo Vespucci** was commissioned by Spain and discovered the coast of what is now known as South America. Shortly thereafter, the word "America" was used to describe the New World.
- **Ponce de Leon** landed in Florida in 1513 near the present city of Saint Augustine and proclaimed that he had found the "fountain of youth."
- In 1540 **Francisco Coronado** attempted to find the mythical Seven Cities of Cibola. Instead, his journey from Mexico took him to the Grand Canyon and Kansas.
- In 1541 **Hernando de Soto** of Spain navigated the Mississippi River. This important water route became a major artery for future settlement.
- By 1565 the first Spanish settlers had made a permanent home in Saint Augustine after **Pedro Menendez** established it when Spain drove the French out of Florida.

French exploration

- Italian sailor **Giovanni da Verrazzano** was hired by France and made landfall in North Carolina in 1524. Then he sailed north along the Atlantic Coast past New York.
- Frenchman **Jacques Cartier** left Europe and instead of finding Asia, discovered the Saint Lawrence Seaway in 1535. By the sixteenth century, France had laid claim to North America.

English exploration

Though getting a late start, England became a dominant player in exploration. In 1578 **Humphrey Gilbert**, after receiving a commission from Queen Elizabeth I, began the search for the Northwest Passage. He was lost at sea, and in 1585 his half-brother **Walter Raleigh** continued the journey and established the first British colony off the coast of North Carolina. It proved to be a failure.

Events in Europe caused a major shift in world leadership as England defeated the Spanish Armada in 1588. This event established England as the new world power and gave them an advantage in creating and maintaining colonies in the New World.

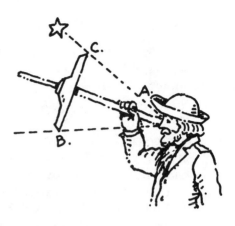

EYEWITNESS ACCOUNT: VERRAZZANO'S DIARY

The people are almost like unto the others, and clad with feather of fowls of diverse colors. They came towards us very cheerfully, making great shouts of admiration, showing us where we might come to land most safely with our boat. We entered up the said river into the land about half a league, where it made a most pleasant lake [the Upper bay] about 3 leagues in compass; on the which they rowed from the one side to the other, to the number of 30 in their small boats, wherein were many people, which passed from one shore to the other to come and see us. And behold, upon the sudden (as it is wont to fall out in sailing) a contrary flaw of wind coming from the sea, we were enforced to return to our ship, leaving this land, to our great discontentment for the great commodity and pleasantness thereof, which we suppose is not without some riches, all the hills showing mineral matters in them.

What were Verrazzano's first impressions when he entered the harbor? What do you think his reaction would be today?

Here you can actually paint a picture in your mind of what Verrazzano saw: the tides of New York Harbor, the first meeting with the inhabitants, the Native Americans, and the great potential of the land. If Verrazzano were alive today, he would be astonished to see the bridge named after him. He would certainly find it very difficult to understand modern-day New York City.

THE NEW WORLD DEVELOPS SETTLEMENTS

By 1600 the era of European migration to the North American continent was well underway. The settlers chose geographic areas first discovered by their country's explorers. Spanish colonies had been established in Mexico, the West Indies, South America, and Florida. The French settled in parts of Canada. The Dutch established a home base in what is now New York City. The country that had the most influence and quickly emerged as the dominant colonizer was England.

Voyages to the New World took six to twelve weeks in small overcrowded ships. Many settlers died of disease and some ships were lost at sea. The reasons why Europeans left their homeland varied, and included:

political oppression
lack of freedom to practice their religion
economic hardship

Let's look at three early colonies:

Jamestown, named after King James I, based on a charter that granted the Virginia Company the right to settle the area.
Massachusetts Bay Colony, settled by the Puritans in 1620.
New Netherland, established by Henry Hudson in 1609.

Jamestown

After receiving a charter from King James I, around 100 men set out for the New World and established Jamestown in 1607. They were really interested in finding gold, but had to settle on farming to make a living. A leader by the name of Captain John Smith became the head of the colony. He had to face attacks from Indians as well as starvation. After he returned to England, the colony fell apart because of smallpox. Of the 300 original colonists, only 60 survived.

The turning point for Jamestown came in 1612 when tobacco became a major export and began to make the colony prosperous. Though this product brought more people to the colony, the death rate from disease and Indian attacks was high. From a peak of 14,000 inhabitants, the colony had only 1,132 people in 1624 when it was officially made a royal colony.

HISTORICAL TIDBIT

Even as early as 1588 there were indications that tobacco was unhealthy. Thomas Hariot wrote in *A Brief and True Report of the New Found Land of Virginia* of the potential danger of tobacco to the body.

Virginia's view of Jamestown:
> *The Far East has its Mecca, Palestine its Jersualem, France its Lourdes, and Italy its Loretto, but America's only shrines are her altars of patriotism — the first and most potent being Jamestown; the sire of Virginia, and Virginia the mother of this great Republic.*
> *—from a 1907 Virginia guidebook*

Massachusetts Bay Colony

This colony was developed primarily by a group called the Puritans. They were very unhappy about religious practices and persecution in England and organized a group called **"Separatists."**

 Separatists–A radical group of Puritans who did not feel that the Church of England could be reformed. They received a land grant from the Virginia Company and set out for the New World in 1620.

The Puritan group boarded *The Mayflower* and after facing a terrible storm that sent their ship off course, they landed in Cape Cod. The group, better known as the Pilgrims, named the colony Plymouth.

 **HISTORICAL TIDBIT**

Though named after Plymouth, England, Prince Charles gave the name Plymouth to the area where the Pilgrims landed years before they ever set sail.

After landing, the Pilgrims signed an agreement to form a government in 1620 that had "just and equal laws." This agreement became known as the Mayflower Compact.

In their first winter, the Puritans faced extreme conditions and many died. By the next fall, they were helped by the Wampanoag Indians who taught them how to plant and grow maize. Our national holiday of Thanksgiving is an outgrowth of the successful fall harvest.

The Massachusetts Bay Colony played an important role in early colonial history. It is interesting to note that even though the Puritans left England protesting religious persecution, they set forth strict religious rules in the new colony. Because of these rules, some Puritans, such as Roger Williams, left Massachusetts and started a settlement in Providence, Rhode Island, in 1636, where he allowed complete religious freedom.

EYEWITNESS ACCOUNT

Letter of William Hilton to His Family:

(William Hilton came to Plymouth on the ship *Fortune* in 1621).

Loving Cousin,

At our arrival at New Plymouth, in New England, we found all our friends and planters in good health, though they were left sick and weak, with very small means; the Indians round about us peaceable and friendly; the country very pleasant and temperate, yielding naturally, of itself, great store of fruits, as vines of divers sorts, in great abundance. There is likewise walnuts, chestnuts, small nuts and plums, with much variety of flowers, roots and herbs, no less pleasant than wholesome and profitable. No place hath more gooseberries and strawberries, nor better. Timer of all sorts you have in England doth cover the land, that affords beasts of divers sorts, and great flocks of turkeys, quails, pigeons and partridges; many great lakes abounding with fish, fowl, beavers, and otters. The sea affords us great plenty of all excellent sorts of sea-fish, as the rivers and isles doth variety of wild fowl of most useful sorts. Mines we find, to our thinking; but neither the goodness nor quality we know. Better grain cannot be than the Indian corn, if we will plant it upon as good ground as a man need desire. We are all freeholders; the rent-day doth not trouble us; and all those good blessings we have, of which and what we list in their seasons for taking. Our company are, for the most part, very religious, honest people; the word of God sincerely taught us ever Sabbath; so that I know not any thing a contented mind can here want. I desire your friendly care to send my wife and children to me, where I wish all the friends I have in England; and so I rest

Your loving kinsman,
William Hilton

How did William Hilton describe conditions at New Plymouth?

New Netherland

Named by Henry Hudson, who explored the area around what is now New York City in 1609, the Dutch East India Company laid claim to it. The company's interest was fur trade and the settlers developed a relationship with the Five Nations of the Iroquois.

The settlement grew in the early 1620s, and in 1624 the island was obtained from the Indians by Peter Minuit for the ridiculously low price of $24. The Dutch form of government was very different from that of the English. They set up what was known as a **patroon system**.

Patroon system—Set up by the Dutch in New Netherland and based on the feudal system of aristocrats owning the land and a lower class working the land.

THE FIRST SLAVES

Remember, the title of this chapter is "Three Worlds Collide." These worlds are those of the Europeans, the Native American Indians, and the African slaves. So far, we have described Native Americans as the first inhabitants of North America and we have looked at the Europeans and their quest for exploration. Now let's see what happened when slavery was introduced to the New World.

The first black slaves were brought into the New World in Jamestown, Virginia, in 1619, just twelve years after its founding. Slavery existed in African society, long before Europe even began to trade with Africa. The Portuguese began European slave trading in 1441 when a ship returned from Africa with its cargo of slaves. Slavery quickly became a way of life. By the end of the fifteenth century, Portugal became the center for trade in African goods and slaves. We will return to this subject in more detail in the next chapter.

COLONIAL-INDIAN RELATIONS

The final section of Sherlock's look at the beginnings of American history tie together two of the worlds that met in this new land: the European colonists and the Native American Indians.

You can imagine that for many Indians the increased number of white settlers would pose a threat. Even though there was cooperation, such as we saw with the Pilgrims, there were many conflicts. An example occurred in Virginia in 1622 when there was an Indian uprising and over 300 whites were killed, including missionaries.

As the European settlers moved deeper into the interior of the Eastern colonies, they became a greater threat to the Indians. Animal game was killed off by the settlers and, of course, the Indians resisted these advances. The Iroquois nation was the most successful in stopping further movement into their territory. In 1570 the Indians formed an organization called the League of the Iroquois. It consisted of a council that had the ability to pass laws. It also set up trading agreements and became a key player in what was known as the French and Indian War of 1754–1763. We will look more closely at this relationship between the Europeans and Indians in future chapters.

SHERLOCK'S MATCHING MADNESS

Match each explorer with the place he discovered.

Amerigo Vespucci	Saint Lawrence Seaway
Ponce de Leon	Grand Canyon
Francisco Coronado	Saint Lawrence Seaway
Hernando de Soto	Saint Augustine
Pedro Menendez	Mississippi River
Giovanni da Verrazzano	Northwest Passage
Jacques Cartier	New York Harbor
Walter Raleigh	Florida
Humphrey Gilbert	Jamestown

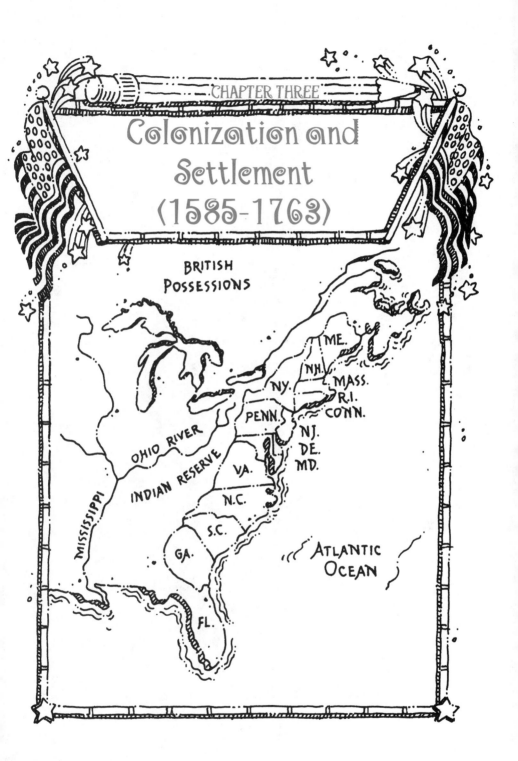

CHAPTER THREE

Colonization and Settlement (1585-1763)

BRITISH
POSSESSIONS

ME.

NH.

MASS.

NY.

R.I.

CONN.

PENN.

NJ.

DE.

MD.

OHIO RIVER

VA.

INDIAN RESERVE

N.C.

MISSISSIPPI

S.C.

GA.

ATLANTIC
OCEAN

FL.

Political power, then, I take to be a right of making laws . . . for the public good.
        —John Locke on the true original extent and end of civil government, 1690

Time Line (1619–1754)

1619 House of Burgesses founded

1630 The Massachusetts Bay Colony founded

1634 Maryland founded

1636 Roger Williams leads a settlement to Providence, Rhode Island

1638 Anne Hutchinson ordered to leave Massachusetts

1652 Rhode Island passes the first laws protecting the treatment of slaves

1660 The Navigation Act passed

1672 The Royal Africa Company gets exclusive rights to the English slave trade to the New World

1675 King Philip's War breaks out

1676 Bacon's Rebellion erupts

1681 Pennsylvania founded by William Penn

1684 The Massachusetts Bay Colony charter taken back by King Charles II

1690 King William's War breaks out

1690 John Locke writes an *Essay Concerning Human Rights*

1692 The Salem witch trials reach a frenzy

1696 Quakers forbid the importing of slaves

1696 The Royal African Trade Company loses its exclusive right to trade slaves

1705 Virginia passes a law stating that black slaves were to remain in servitude for life

1711 The Tuscarora Indian War breaks out in North Carolina

1718 New Orleans founded by the French

1720 The colonial population grows to over 400,000 people

1725 The population of African slaves grows to 75,000

1729 Benjamin Franklin begins the publication of *The Pennsylvania Gazette*

1732 Georgia chartered; Franklin publishes *Poor Richard's Almanack*

1734 John Peter Zenger tried for libel

1744 The Great Awakening religious movement

1754 The French and Indian War

PATTERNS OF COLONIZATION

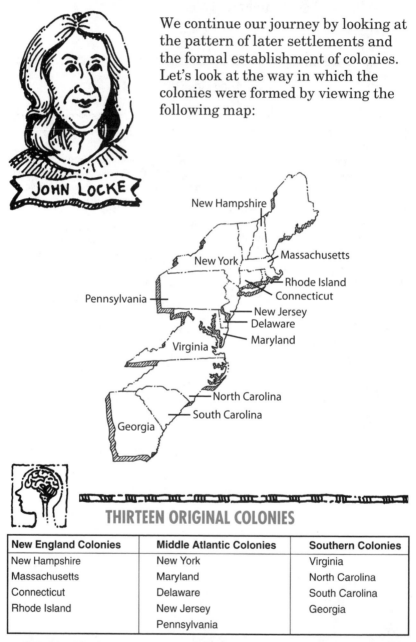

JOHN LOCKE

We continue our journey by looking at the pattern of later settlements and the formal establishment of colonies. Let's look at the way in which the colonies were formed by viewing the following map:

New Hampshire

New York

Massachusetts

Rhode Island
Connecticut

Pennsylvania

New Jersey
Delaware
Maryland

Virginia

North Carolina
South Carolina

Georgia

THIRTEEN ORIGINAL COLONIES

New England Colonies	Middle Atlantic Colonies	Southern Colonies
New Hampshire	New York	Virginia
Massachusetts	Maryland	North Carolina
Connecticut	Delaware	South Carolina
Rhode Island	New Jersey	Georgia
	Pennsylvania	

Find the New England colonies, the Middle Atlantic colonies, and the southern colonies.

Sherlock emphasizes geography because it is an important factor in understanding the economics of colonization. Because of the economic opportunity, you will also see a tremendous influx of people coming from Europe. These immigrants included a large percentage of English people; however, there were also Dutch, French, Spaniards, and, of course, slaves from Africa. Let's break down each geographic area and look at how the geography influenced the economy of the region.

The New England colonies

Because of the severe winter climate and the lack of good land for farming, the New England colonists turned to shipbuilding and trading, and established the beginnings of a factory system. By the middle of the seventeenth century, the Massachusetts Bay Company established itself as a central force. Boston Harbor became one of the best-known ports. One third of the British fleet was built in New England. New Englanders also took advantage of the slave trade by participating in what became known as the **Triangular Trade**.

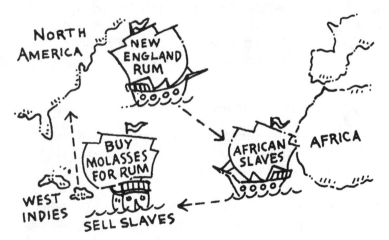

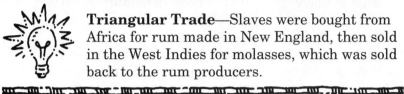

Triangular Trade—Slaves were bought from Africa for rum made in New England, then sold in the West Indies for molasses, which was sold back to the rum producers.

We will deal more with this later in the chapter.

The Middle Atlantic colonies

If your focus your attention on Pennsylvania and New York, you will be able to see the influence that Europeans, especially the Scots and Irish, had on these colonies. In Pennsylvania, which was founded by William Penn in 1681, the geography of its largest city, Philadelphia, reflected a city soon to be called the "city of brotherly love." Based on a Quaker tradition, Pennsylvania houses were made of brick and stone. Philadelphia also had many busy docks and it pursued trade. The population grew to over 30,000 people by 1776.

New York was originally founded by the Dutch and sold to them by the Native American inhabitants for the meager sum of $24. It became the home of many Europeans—French, Danes, Norwegians, Swedes, English, Scots, Irish, and Germans. Even after the British gained control of the colony, it continued to have a strong Dutch influence. New York City also became the center for trade.

The southern colonies

The South was much different in geography as well as economic interests from New England and the Middle Atlantic colonies. Virginia, Maryland, North Carolina, South Carolina, and later, Georgia were mostly rural. Large plantations were built. Big landowners held much of the political power, and they were supported by slaves.

Charleston, South Carolina, became one of the largest trading centers in the South. Unlike their northern cousins, people living in the South combined the benefits of agriculture and commerce. Tobacco became a major crop, especially in Virginia. In the other southern colonies rice and indigo were produced; later, cotton became the major southern product, supported by slave labor.

European influences in the South included German immigrants and Scot-Irish, as well as English settlers. Living within these colonies and certainly outside their borders were numerous Native American tribes.

 ## HISTORICAL TIDBITS

- New England—Governor John Winthrop of Massachusetts wanted to create a "Puritan Utopia" for the region.
- Middle Atlantic—William Penn wanted to start a "holy experiment" for the region.
- Southern Colonies—In pursuing his rebellion, Nathaniel Bacon pledged to "wage war against all Indians in general."

If you want to get a sense of how life was in the thirteen original colonies, ask your parents to plan a trip that could include Mystic Seaport, Connecticut; Boston, Massachusetts; and Newport, Rhode Island. These places have maintained their colonial heritage:

- **Mystic Seaport, Connecticut**—You can visit a museum that has an eighteenth-century flavor. In downtown Mystic, there are many privately owned homes that were built during the colonial period.
- **Boston, Massachusetts**—You can visit some of the famous sites of the colonial period including Bunker Hill and a museum commemorating the Boston Tea Party. You can also take a walk along the Freedom Trail.
- **Newport, Rhode Island**—You can see the Friends Meeting House, built in 1699. It is the oldest religious building in Newport and features the history of the Quakers, once the dominant religion in Newport. Speaking of religion, you can also see the Touro synagogue, the oldest Jewish house of worship in America.

POLITICAL INSTITUTIONS IN THE ENGLISH COLONIES

In this section, you will be looking closely at the way in which the colonists attempted to balance their desire for self-government with England's need to control the colonists.

CHAPTER FLASHBACK

In Chapter Two, you explored the significance of the Mayflower Compact, signed in 1620 as a means for self-government. You also established the fact that one key reason for colonization was political oppression in England.

Look at the Time Line at the beginning of the chapter. Decide if the event contributed to political freedom or if it restricted the development of representative government in the colonies.

In order to evaluate whether an event had a positive or negative political impact, you must measure the extent it contributed to democratic values. These include representation, the right to vote, the right to protest peaceably, and the right to engage in free trade.

- **The House of Burgesses**—Contributed to democratic values because it increased representation.
- **The Fundamental Orders of Connecticut**— Contributed to democratic values because it increased representation.
- **New England Confederation**—Contributed to democratic values because it moved the colonies towards democracy.
- **The Navigation Act**—Restricted democratic values because England controlled free trade.
- **Bacon's Rebellion**—Restricted democratic values because the rebellion was not successful and violence was used.

- **Zenger's Trial**—Contributed to democratic values because it helped establish freedom of the press.

Let's take a look at the political picture of the colonies:

- In 1619 the first meeting of the **House of Burgesses** took place.

House of Burgesses—The first representative assembly. It met in Virginia.

It was significant that the people of Virginia were able to freely elect representatives who could pass laws.
- In 1639 the Fundamental Orders of Connecticut were passed. This document also established a representative assembly for Connecticut. The ideas were also picked up by Rhode Island.
- The New England Confederation was established in 1643. Consisting of Massachusetts Bay, Plymouth, Connecticut, and New Haven colonies, it was the first attempt to form a regional organization.
- The Navigation Act was passed by England in 1660. This act established a **mercantilist** policy.

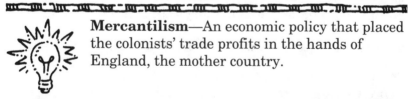

Mercantilism—An economic policy that placed the colonists' trade profits in the hands of England, the mother country.

- Bacon's Rebellion broke out in Virginia in 1675. Nathaniel Bacon, a Virginia farmer, organized an armed uprising against Virginia Governor William Berkeley over the issues of low tobacco prices and difficult living conditions. Berkeley refused to give in to the demands, but he did agree to hold new elections for the House of Burgesses. After winning a series of victories and gaining the support of many of the farmers, Bacon died and the rebellion was crushed. Berkeley punished Bacon's followers by hanging twenty-three rebels.

- Individuals also added to a political climate that viewed democratic values in a positive way. English philosopher John Locke wrote a series of essays including an *Essay Concerning Human Rights.* In this essay, he stressed the need for natural rights, the right of people to enjoy the freedom of life, liberty, and property.

- The Glorious Revolution in England (1688–1689) had many positive effects on the British colonies. Though it established the supremacy of the English Parliament over the colonies, the colonists were able to use some of the powers of Parliament. They made laws such as the right to vote on taxes and the right to pass legislation.

- A young lawyer named Andrew Hamilton struck a blow for freedom of the press in 1734. He defended John Peter Zenger who was accused of *libel*—which is making false statements—against the colonial governor of New York. Zenger was found not guilty, and an early principle of freedom of the press was established.

 HISTORICAL TIDBIT

Lawyers were looked down upon during colonial times. Massachusetts Bay and Virginia both passed laws making it difficult for lawyers to practice.

Create your own blog, a web diary, where you can write your own comments regarding colonial political life and get feedback from your classmates. You can find many sites on the Internet that walk you through creating a blog (key word search: create blog).

When you participate in a blog, you must follow rules of conduct such as:

1. Be civil. Your postings will be monitored.
2. Write clearly so that what you write is easy to understand.

3. Do not use obscene language; it will not be tolerated.
4. Follow the format when you create a new posting.

HISTORICAL TIDBIT
Colonial Connecticut passed laws that resulted in severe penalties against children older than 15 years who committed the crime of cursing against their natural mother or father; death was a penalty, unless it could be proven that the parent did not sufficiently provide an education for the children.

RELIGIOUS INSTITUTIONS IN THE ENGLISH COLONIES

CHAPTER FLASHBACK

In Chapter Two you explored the early exploration of the New World because of religious persecution in England. The groups that were affected were the Puritans who settled in Massachusetts, and a group that broke away from the Puritans, led by Roger Williams, which set up a colony in Rhode Island.

As you saw earlier in this chapter, other religious groups became strong influences in the colonies. One such group was the Quakers, who settled Pennsylvania. But, even with these religious influences, the status of religion in later colonial history ranged from attempts to guarantee religious freedom to ugly acts of religious persecution.

S I N N E R S
In the hands of an
Angry GOD.
A SERMON

Let's evaluate how the following events pertained positively or negatively to religious freedom. You must measure the extent to which each event allowed for the free exercise of religion and the extent to which government did not impose its own religion.

Time line (1634–1728)

1634—Maryland accepted Catholics—Contributed positively because it allowed the free exercise of religion.

1638—Anne Hutchinson—Massachusetts restricted religious freedom.

1646—Death penalty to those who didn't follow Puritanism—Restricted religious freedom because the government imposed a religion.

1649—The Toleration Act—Contributed to religious freedom because it allowed the free exercise of different religions.

1660—Mary Dyer banished and then hung—Restricted religious freedom because the state imposed a death penalty.

1667—William Penn's charter—Contributed to religious freedom because it encouraged the **separation of Church and State**.

Separation of Church and State—The doctrine that makes it illegal for the government to impose an official religion on individuals.

1692—The Salem witch trials—Restricted religious freedom because the state allowed executions of those thought to be practicing a different religion.

1702—The Anglican Church made the official religion in Maryland—Restricted religious freedom because the government was imposing a religion.

1728—Jewish Synagogue built in New York—Contributed to religious freedom because it encouraged different religious practices.

1741—The Great Awakening—Restricted religious freedom because the sermon preached that there is only one acceptable religion.

http://www.lcweb.loc.gov/exhibits/religion/religion.html

Before we leave the area of religion, you should also explore in more detail the Salem witch trials, one of the most terrifying events in American history. It was popularized in the play by Arthur Miller and later, the movie, *The Crucible*.

HISTORICAL TIDBIT

The New York Times reported in 1976 that the people accused of witchcraft in Salem could have possibly been hallucinating as a result of eating tainted bread that contained an ingredient similar to LSD.

THE SALEM WITCH TRIAL ROLE-PLAYING ACTIVITY: YOU BE THE JUDGE:

Read the evidence of the Salem Witch Trial against Sarah Good and you decide whether there should be a guilty or innocent verdict.

Saw Good [ther] practice witchcraft
Saw Good have a Catt besides the bird & a thing all over hair [ther]
Sarah Good appeared like a wolfe to Hubbard going to proctors & saw it sent by Good to Hubbard

good [ther] hurt the Children again & the Children
affirme the same Hubbard knew th[em] not being blinded
by them & was once or twice taken dumb herslefe i:e:
Titube
Good cause her to pinch the Children in their own
persons
Saw Goods name in the booke, & the devell told her
they made these marks & said to her she made ther marke
& it was the same day she went to prison
Good [ther] came to ride abroad with her & the man
shewed her Goods mark in the book
Good [ther] pinched her on the leggs & being searched
found it soe after confession
Nota S. G. mumbled when she went away from Mr
Parrass & the children after hurt

If you want to explore further the Salem Witch Trials, you
can visit the Salem Witch Museum in Salem, Massachusetts,
and visit the museum on the Internet at:

http://www.salemwitchmuseum.com

SOCIAL INSTITUTIONS
OF THE ENGLISH COLONIES

The last part of this chapter deals with the development of
cultural institutions in the colonies.

CHAPTER FLASHBACK

If you remember, the beginnings of the colonial
culture took place as the new settlers brought
their own culture from Europe. They also
adopted many of the traditions of the Native Americans.

Let's look at the Time Line and locate the following cultural events. How did these events contribute to the development of colonial culture?

Time line (1631–1742)

1631—The first Thanksgiving celebrated → holiday

1636—Harvard College founded → education

1638—The first almanac describing life in the colonies published → popular entertainment

1647—The first public education law put into place in Massachusetts → education

1658—The first hospital set up in New Amsterdam → social issue

1660—Marriage laws passed in Connecticut and other colonies → social issue

1690—The first newspaper published in Boston. It only survives for four days since it did not have the permission of the government to publish → popular entertainment

1701—Yale founded in Connecticut → education

1732—*Poor Richard's Almanack* was published by Benjamin Franklin → popular entertainment

Here is an example of an entry in the *Almanack:*

When you're good to others,
  you are best to yourself.
Half Wits talk much but say
  little.
If Jack's in love, he's no judge
  of Jill's Beauty.
Most Fools think they are only
  ignorant.

1742—The Franklin Stove invented → science

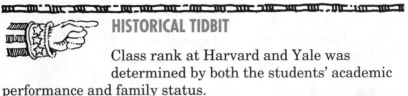

HISTORICAL TIDBIT

Class rank at Harvard and Yale was determined by both the students' academic performance and family status.

To further illustrate the nature of colonial culture, let's focus our attention on one of the most influential people— Benjamin Franklin. He would play a significant role during and after the American Revolution.

BEN FRANKLIN'S ACCOMPLISHMENTS

Science—Noted eighteenth-century scientist

Inventing—Stove, lightning rod, bifocals, and many others

Medicine—Founded first U.S. hospital

Printing—Noted colonial printer—"Patron Saint of Printing"

Electricity—Experiments and theories—kite & key

Heating—Franklin stove

Education—Involved in founding two colleges

Optometrics—Bifocal glasses

Public safety—Started first police department

Public safety II—Started first fire department

Government—Held numerous positions:
- Clerk
- Postmaster
- J.P.
- Alderman
- Governor
- Ambassador

Diplomacy—Ambassador to England and minister to France

Community service—Street lighting, paving and cleaning

Abolitionism—Started Society to Abolish Slavery

Sales—Expert at marketing and sales

Merchandising—Operated store as part of printshop

Forecasting—Published *Poor Richards Almanack*

Sailing—Designed "sea anchors"

Cartoonist—Drew first cartoon in an American newspaper

Linguist—Studied several languages and designed a phonetic alphabet

Cartographer—Mapped the Gulf Stream and Routes for the post office

Philanthropist—Organized fund raising and contributed to many worthwhile causes

THE STATUS OF SLAVERY AND ITS IMPACT ON COLONIAL LIFE

Slavery continued to play an increasingly important role in both the New England and southern colonies.

CHAPTER FLASHBACK

Remember, slaves were first bought by the Portuguese and soon thereafter brought to the New World. A triangle trade was set up for the benefit of New Englanders, and the South began to use slaves on their farms.

Let's take a look at why slavery increased and the attempts by some to limit it.

Look at the Time Line and locate the events that impacted on the development of slavery in the colonies.

Which events could be classified as positive? Which events can be classified as negative?

Time line (1652–1739)

1652—The Dutch government approves exporting African slaves → negative

1652—Rhode Island passes laws protecting the treatment of slaves → positive

1664—Maryland passes a slavery act. It provides for the lifelong status of slaves. Similar laws passed in other colonies → negative

1672—Royal African Trade Company obtains exclusive rights to the English slave trade in the New World → negative

1696—The Quakers outlaw importing slaves → positive

1696—The Royal African Trade Company loses its exclusive right to trade slaves → negative

1725—Slave population reaches 75,000 → negative

1739—Three slave uprisings break out in South Carolina → positive

 HISTORICAL TIDBIT

Individual slaves had many stories. One slave reported that he was whipped because his owner wanted to punish the master's wife for whipping a slave after the owner told her not to.

EYEWITNESS ACCOUNT

The slaves are put in stalls like . . . cattle.
— James Martin

James Martin, born on a Virginia plantation in 1847, was 90 years old when he was interviewed by the Works Progress Administration in 1937. After the Civil War he moved to Texas, where he served in the 9th U.S. Cavalry and later worked as a cowboy. Here, he describes a slave auction.

The slaves are put in stalls like the pens they use for cattle—a man and his wife with a child on each arm. And

there's a curtain, sometimes just a sheet over the front of the stall, so the bidders can't see the "stock" too soon. The overseer's standin' just outside with a big black snake whip and a pepperbox pistol in his belt. Across the square a little piece, there's a big platform with steps leadin' to it.

Then, they pulls up the curtain, and the bidders is crowdin' around. Them in back can't see, sot he overseer drives the slaves out to the platform, and he tells the ages of the slaves and what they can do. They have white gloves there, and one of the bidders takes a pair of globes and rubs his fingers over a man's teeth, and he says to the overseer, "You call this buck twenty years old? Why there's cut worms in his teeth. He's forty years old, if he's a day." So they knock this buck down for a thousand dollars. They calls the men "bucks" and the women "wenches."

When the slaves is on the platform—what they calls the "block"—the overseer yells, "Tom or Jason, show the bidders how you walk." Then, the slave steps across the platform, and the biddin' starts.

Sherlock's Question: Why were the slaves treated so harshly?

The issue of slavery caused much controversy even in the early days of colonization. Northerners felt that slavery was wrong, while in the South, plantation owners saw the need for what they called "the peculiar institution."

SHERLOCK'S HEADLINE HUNT:

Fill in the blank that completes the headline.

The House of Burgesses
The Fundamental Orders of Connecticut
The New England Confederation
The Navigation Act
Nathaniel Bacon
John Peter Zenger

1. _____ found innocent of libel charges made by New York colonial Governor.

2. The first representative assembly, _____, was formed in Virgina.

3. A Virginia farmer, _____, organized an armed uprising over the issues of low tobacco prices and difficult living conditions.

4. _____ restricts colonial free trade.

5. The first written colonial constitution, _____, was adopted.

6. Colonies in Massachusetts and Connecticut form _____ _____.

CHAPTER FOUR

Revolution and the New Nation (1754-1820)

These are the times that try men's souls.

—Thomas Paine, 1776

Time Line (1754–1791)

1754 Albany Congress convenes

1756 England declares war on France in Europe

1760 King George III crowned

1763 Treaty of Paris signed

1763 Proclamation of 1763

1764 Sugar Act passed

1764 Currency Act passed

1765 Stamp Act passed

1765 Quartering Act passed

1765 Sons of Liberty formed

1765 Stamp Act Congress meets in New York City

1766 Repeal of Stamp Act

1766 English Parliament passes Declaratory Acts

1767 The Townshend Acts passed

1770 Boston Massacre

1770 British Captain Thomas Preston found not guilty in his role in the Boston Massacre

1772 Boston Committee of Correspondence formed

1773 Tea Act goes into effect

1773 Boston patriots dump tea in Boston Harbor in what is known as the Boston Tea Party

1774 Coercive Acts, also known as Intolerable Acts, passed

1774 First Continental Congress meets

1775 Paul Revere warns colonists that "the British are coming!"

1775 Battles of Lexington and Concord

1775 Second Continental Congress

1775 Battle of Bunker Hill

1775 George Washington made commander of colonial troops

1776 Thomas Paine publishes *Common Sense*

1776 Declaration of Independence passed

1776 States draft individual constitutions

1781 Articles of Confederation ratified

1785 Congress establishes dollar as official currency

1786 Shays' Rebellion

1787 Northwest Ordinance

1787 Constitutional Convention meets

1788 Federalist Papers

1789 Constitution ratified

1789 Washington sworn in as first president

1791 Bill of Rights added to Constitution

THE CAUSES OF THE
AMERICAN REVOLUTION

Sherlock begins the story about one of the greatest
accomplishments in American history—the founding of the
new nation. As you look at the events that caused loyal British
colonists to take up arms against the strongest country in the
world, imagine what dangers and risks they faced, especially
if the rebellion was crushed. There was no doubt that the
rebels, who were fighting for what they believed was a just
cause, were traitors in the minds of the British.

CHAPTER FLASHBACK

Think back to the development of the colonies
in the late seventeenth and early eighteenth
centuries. All of the colonies had established
democratic traditions based on a model of representative
government. Ideas from the Magna Carta, institutions like
the House of Burgesses, and traditions that came from the
Mayflower Compact became part of colonial life.

Relations with Native Americans also had a positive
impact on colonial development. One key event that helped
solidify this relationship was the French and Indian War,
which started in 1754. Because of previous intercolonial wars
between the English and French such as King William's
War (1689–1697), Queen Anne's War (1701–1713), and King
George's War (1744–1748), the colonists came up with a plan
known as the **Albany Plan of Union**.

Albany Plan of Union—An idea developed
by Benjamin Franklin in which the colonies of
Maryland, Pennsylvania, New York, and New
England would join together and make laws.

The king rejected the idea and the colonies remained separated during the next great war. Named the French and Indian War, also known as the Seven Years War, it quickly spread into Europe. Though the French had the support of many Indian tribes, it was significant that because of the Albany Plan of Union, the Iroquois remained loyal to the British. The war finally ended in 1763 with the signing of the Treaty of Paris. This treaty had the following provisions:

- Great Britain took possession of Canada and the lands east of the Mississippi River.
- England also got Florida from Spain because Spain helped France in the war.
- France no longer was a colonial power in North America.

HISTORY COMES ALIVE AT THE FORT WILLIAM HENRY MUSEUM

You can visit the Fort William Henry Museum in Lake George, New York. It is the site that was destroyed in the French and Indian War and has been transformed into an historical site. A massacre at the fort was described by an eyewitness:

This Day when they Came to march the Savage Indiens Came upon them and Stript them of their Packs and Cloths and the most of their Arms then they Pickt out the negrows Melatows and Indiens and Dragd them Away and we Know not what is Become of them then they fell to killing of our men At A most Dredfull manner they Ravesht the women and then Put them to the Slaughter young Children of the Regular forces had their Brains Dasht out Against the Stones and trees

Sherlock's Question: How would you feel about the Indians after reading this account of the massacre?

KING GEORGE III

After the treaty went into effect, the history of the colonies went into a new phase. One reason for the colonists' uneasiness was the fact that there was a new king in England—King George III. Unlike past monarchs, this king had a different point of view about the way he would rule over the colonies.

So you say you want a revolution—take the role of a colonist.

Look at the two Mind Map outlines that describe the political and economic causes of the American Revolution. Check out the Time Line at the beginning of the chapter.

Imagine life under the rule of King George III. Then, decide what to do after the king imposed a series of acts that changed the way of life for the colonists. The organization that was formed to take action against these acts was called the Sons of Liberty; it eventually evolved into a more revolutionary group. Historically, each act provoked a reaction from the colonists. Weigh in your own mind how serious you feel these acts were in deciding what actions you would take. Look at the Mind Maps and the Time Line. Pick the most significant event. This becomes one of the key turning points in determining the main cause of the American Revolution.

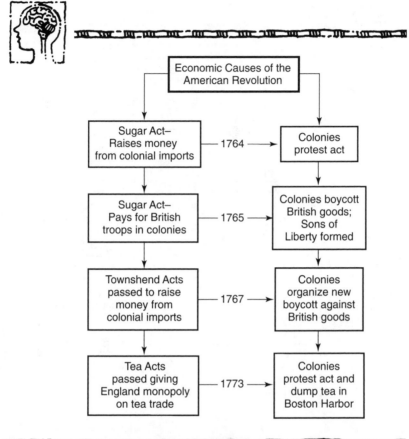

Economic Causes of the American Revolution

Sugar Act– Raises money from colonial imports	— 1764 →	Colonies protest act
Sugar Act– Pays for British troops in colonies	— 1765 →	Colonies boycott British goods; Sons of Liberty formed
Townshend Acts passed to raise money from colonial imports	— 1767 →	Colonies organize new boycott against British goods
Tea Acts passed giving England monopoly on tea trade	— 1773 →	Colonies protest act and dump tea in Boston Harbor

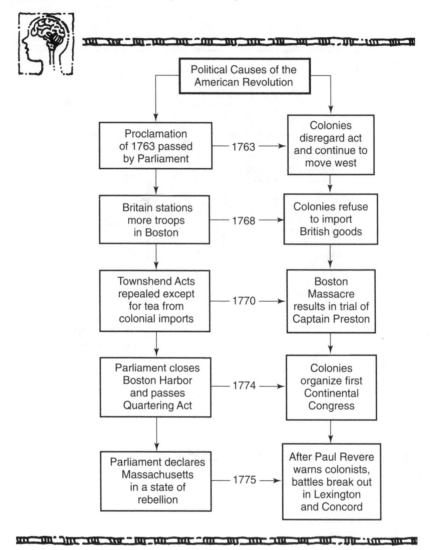

Political Causes of the American Revolution		
Proclamation of 1763 passed by Parliament	1763 →	Colonies disregard act and continue to move west
Britain stations more troops in Boston	1768 →	Colonies refuse to import British goods
Townshend Acts repealed except for tea from colonial imports	1770 →	Boston Massacre results in trial of Captain Preston
Parliament closes Boston Harbor and passes Quartering Act	1774 →	Colonies organize first Continental Congress
Parliament declares Massachusetts in a state of rebellion	1775 →	After Paul Revere warns colonists, battles break out in Lexington and Concord

New British control over the colonies

Beginning with the Proclamation of 1763, King George imposed a new, more restrictive way of governing the colonies. Let's take an in-depth look at these measures.

The Proclamation of 1763

This act attempted to stop western expansion by the colonists and reserved the land for the Indian tribes. The measure was never really enforced. The colonists believed they had every right to settle the western territories.

The Sugar Act of 1764

This act replaced the Molasses Act of 1733, which had placed a tax on the import of rum. The new act went one step further and did not allow the colonists to import foreign rum. It also placed a tax on molasses and other items. To enforce this act, Britain instructed its warships to seize smugglers and search the ships using what was called a **writ of assistance.**

 Writs of assistance—Search warrants issued by the king that allowed British warships to search any ship for smuggled goods, even if there was no probable cause.

Currency Act of 1764

This act prevented the use of any colonial currency as legal tender; therefore any colonial money would have no legal value.

Quartering Act of 1765

This act required colonies to provide British troops with provisions and a home while they were stationed in the colonies.

Stamp Act of 1765

This was the harshest provision of the first series of acts imposed on the colonies. It provided that stamps in the form of a tax had to be placed on many colonial documents. The act was resisted in the colonies, and men organized the "Sons of Liberty," a secret

organization opposed to the Stamp Act. Colonial assemblies passed laws rejecting the tax. Patrick Henry, in a very famous speech in the Virginia House of Burgesses, called the act "taxation without representation."

Because it was the first harsh act, the Stamp Act resulted in many colonists driving away the British responsible for collecting the tax. One method of sending a message was to actually pour tar and feathers over individuals. According to the web site, tarring and feathering was used more as a threat against the British tax collectors. As a result, many of them left their posts and did not collect a good portion of the stamp tax.

Declaratory Act (1766)

Though King George III repealed the Stamp Act, that same day the English Parliament passed the Declaratory Act, which declared that the English Parliament was the sole authority to make all laws binding on the colonies.

Townshend Acts (1767)

The first in a series of declared acts of Parliament, the Townshend Acts, named after a British official, established a new set of taxes less harsh than the Stamp Act on imported goods. The citizens of Boston responded by boycotting English luxury items and finding substitutes for imported items. The British increased the number of troops in Boston to protect the customs officials responsible for collecting the taxes.

The Boston Massacre (1770)

With tensions rising, Boston citizens began to snowball British soldiers. The soldiers panicked, and orders were given to fire on the mob. Three Bostonians were killed in the incident, called the Boston Massacre. British Captain Thomas Preston and six of his men were placed on trial. Ironically, colonial leader and lawyer John Adams defended the soldiers and they were acquitted.

Even though the British soldiers were provoked by an angry mob, there was much evidence according to the trial transcript that the British soldiers did give them fair warning before opening fire. The trial of Captain Thomas Preston illustrates that even a colonial patriot like John Adams felt it was important to provide legal counsel.

The Committee of Correspondence (1772)

Organized by Samuel Adams, Massachusetts revolutionary leader, this committee stated the rights and grievances of the colonists. Committees were organized in other colonies and they set the stage for a more organized attempt by the colonies to express their grievances.

Boston Tea Party (1773)

After England, at the urging of the East India Company, passed a tea tax that gave them a monopoly on the tea trade, Samuel Adams and the colonists reacted. They dressed up as Mohawk Indians, boarded three British ships, and dumped the cargo into Boston Harbor.

HISTORICAL TIDBIT

Even with the taxes brought on by the Tea Act, tea still cost less in the colonies than in Britain.

In looking at the boycott led by Boston women after the Tea Party took place, it becomes apparent that colonial women played a significant role in the cause of the Revolution. This will become even clearer when we look at the role Abigail Adams played during the debate over the drafting of the Declaration of Independence.

Coercive Acts (1774)

Called the Intolerable Acts by the colonists, these acts were passed in response to the Boston Tea Party. They closed down the Boston Port to all commercial shipping until Massachusetts agreed to pay the taxes on the dumped tea. Then a new series of acts ended self-rule by the colonists in Massachusetts. In addition, these acts made it illegal to sue royal officials in colonial courts. At the same time, Parliament passed the Quebec Act, which extended the border of Canada into territory claimed by the colonists.

The First Continental Congress (1774)

Created in response to these acts, the first Congress met in Philadelphia and had fifty-six delegates representing all the colonies. Delegates included Patrick Henry, George Washington, Samuel Adams, and John Hancock.

THE IMPACT OF THE AMERICAN REVOLUTION

The Declaration of Independence

Months before July 4, 1776, the country was on an inevitable course that would lead the Second Continental Congress to approve the Declaration of Independence. The King of England could have made concessions or compromised, and the radicals demanding a revolution would have probably been silenced; instead, he took a hard line.

Look at the three key events preceding the passage of the Declaration of Independence: The Battle of Lexington and Concord, the publication of Thomas Paine's *Common Sense,* and the Battle of Bunker Hill. Why should these events be called *defining moments* in the battle for independence?

The term "defining moment" is an important idea when you study history. It means that there is an event that will stand out above the rest, or a phrase that is often quoted. All three events preceding the signing of the Declaration of Independence were defining moments in American history: The Battle of Lexington brought Paul Revere and his midnight ride; the first shots of the Revolution have been called "the shots heard round the world"; the Battle of Bunker Hill brought us the phrase, "Don't shoot until you see the whites of their eyes." In addition, Thomas Paine brought us the memorable phrase, "These are the times that try men's souls."

Lexington and Concord (April 19, 1775)

Before we analyze the battle, look at the first verse of Henry Wadsworth Longfellow's famous poem, "The Midnight Ride of Paul Revere." Imagine what the response of the colonists was when they got the warning, "The British are coming, the British are coming!"

> *Listen, my children,*
>   *and you shall hear*
> *Of the midnight ride of*
>   *Paul Revere,*
> *On the eighteenth of*
>   *April, in*
>   *Seventy-five;*
> *Hardly a man is now*
>   *alive*
> *Who remembers that*
>   *famous day and*
>   *year.*

PAUL REVERE

After Paul Revere warned the colonists, the battle took place at dawn on April 19 when seventy Massachusetts Minutemen confronted the British army on Lexington Green. Eight Americans were killed but the British had to regroup at Concord where they destroyed the colonists' weapons. The event has been called "the shot heard round the world." Shortly after this, the second Continental Congress declared war on Great Britain and appointed George Washington of Virginia as Commander-in-Chief of the American forces.

Battle of Bunker Hill (June 1775)

This was the first key battle of the undeclared war for independence. The American patriots were ordered not to fire until they could see "the whites of their eyes." The British got closer and the battle began. Even though the British succeeded in taking the hill, their loss was much heavier than that of the patriots.

HISTORICAL TIDBIT

Even though it is called the Battle of Bunker Hill, it actually took place on the highest elevation called "Breed's Hill."

Thomas Paine's *Common Sense*

Recently arrived from England, Paine was called a political scientist. He wrote a fifty-page pamphlet called *Common Sense,* which outlined the reasons for separation from Great Britain. It sold over 100,000 copies and laid the groundwork for a Virginian, Thomas Jefferson, to draft one of the most important documents in American history—the Declaration of Independence.

DOCUMENT CHALLENGE

The Declaration of Independence:

When in the Course of human events, it becomes necessary for one people to dissolve

*the political bands which have connected them with
another and to assume among the powers of the earth,
the separate and equal station to which the Laws of
Nature and of Nature's God entitle them, a decent respect
to the opinions of mankind requires that they should
declare the causes which impel them to the separation.*

*We hold these truths to be self-evident; that all men
are created equal, that they are endowed by their Creator
with certain unalienable Rights, that among these are
Life, Liberty, and the pursuit of Happiness.—That, to
secure these rights, Governments are instituted among
Men, deriving their just powers from the consent of the
governed,—That whenever any Form of Government
becomes destructive of these ends, it is the Right of the
People to alter or to abolish it, and to institute new
Government, laying its foundation on such principles, and
organizing its powers in such form, as to them shall seem
most likely to effect their Safety and Happiness.*

Sherlock **Question:** What is the purpose of the opening two
paragraphs of the Declaration of Independence?

A copy of the Declaration of Independence can be viewed
at the National Archives at:

**http://www.archives.gov/exhibits/charters/
declaration.html
Keyword: Declaration of Independence
National Archives**

The signing of the Declaration of Independence was
one of the most memorable events in history. It has been
captured at the National Archives web site. If you make a list
of the original people who signed the document and then find
their signatures, you will be astonished at the differences.
One stands out above the rest—that of John Hancock, who
said he wrote his name so large that King George III would
be able to read it without his glasses.

The importance of the opening of the Declaration points
to the principles of equality, the "natural rights" of "life,
liberty, and the pursuit of happiness," and a government that
is based on citizens having control of who gets elected and
elected officials being responsible to the people.

 HISTORICAL TIDBIT

Though we celebrate Independence Day on July 4, actually the Continental Congress approved the draft of the document two days earlier.

After the Declaration was passed, the war got underway in earnest.

The battle lines

It was obvious from the start that the British had the main advantage in waging the war against the colonists. Their army was well equipped and well trained, and outnumbered the American forces. They also paid 30,000 Germans, called mercenaries, to fight. In addition, they had a number of Loyalists, those colonists who favored Great Britain, including a number of Indian tribes.

The colonists, on the other hand, had the "home court advantage." They were able to fight on land they were familiar with. At a critical point of the war, the French also came to the aid of the colonists. But above all, many believe it was "the spirit of '76" that propelled the colonists to victory.

Look at the following list of battles and their outcomes. Decide what were significant turning points of the Revolutionary War.

Battle and Date	Outcome
Long Island (1776)	British force Washington to flee to Pennsylvania → turning point
Trenton (1777)	Surprise victory for Washington
Saratoga (1777)	Cut off from the rest of the British forces, a major victory is achieved by the colonists → turning point
Valley Forge (1777–1778)	Though not considered a fighting battle, the soldiers under Washington's command suffer terrible hardships
Vincennes (1779)	A major victory for George Rogers Clark in the West; establishes colonial control between the Appalachians and the Mississippi → turning point

THE IMPACT OF THE AMERICAN REVOLUTION

Savannah (1778)	Falls to the British
King's Mountain, Cowpens, South Carolina	Colonial victories
Guilford Courthouse	Americans force British to retreat to Yorktown
Yorktown	British surrender to Washington → turning point

The Treaty of Paris ended the war in 1783 and Great Britain recognized the United States of America. Britain still maintained control of Canada, Spain was given Florida, and both the United States and England had trading rights on the Mississippi.

As you have seen, the decision to become a rebel is a difficult one. In fact, many colonists remained loyal to the British crown and were called Loyalists. They wrote songs criticizing the revolt against the crown. One such song was called "The Rebel."

SHERLOCK CHALLENGE

Look at the last part of the song and explain its point of view:

Come take up you glasses, each true loyal heart,
And may every rebel meet his due dessert,
With his hunting shirt and rifle gun.
May Congress, Conventions, those damned inquisitions,
Be fed with hot sulphur from Lucifer's kitchens,
May commerce and peace again be restored,
And Americans own their true sovereign lord,
Then oblivion to shirts and rifle guns.
GOD SAVE THE KING!

—Lyrics: Captain Smyth, Simcoe's Queen's Rangers
(Originally published in the *Pennsylvania Ledger*, 1778)

The song puts down the efforts of the rebels to break away from the beloved Mother Country.

One event the Loyalists pointed to with pride was the actions of Benedict Arnold. Promising the British the strategic prize of West Point, Arnold fled when his British contact was captured and revealed his plan. Even though Arnold's attempt failed, Loyalists applauded his defection to the British. And to this day if you are called a "turncoat," it is a reference to Arnold's change of uniform and becoming a traitor.

RESULTS OF THE AMERICAN REVOLUTION

Besides gaining independence from the most powerful nation in the world, the colonists also achieved political, social, and economic results.

Political

Each colony formed an individual state; voting rights were based on wealth; women still played a limited role.

Spotlight on Abigail Adams: The wife of John Adams, Abigail wrote a series of letters that pointed out that women should not be overlooked. In one letter she wrote, "Do not push such unlimited power into the hands of their husbands."

Social

Based on the principles of the Declaration of Independence, there was a spirit of equality in the new nation. Immediately following the war, Massachusetts and New Hampshire passed laws ending slavery. Other northern states would soon follow that lead. The situation did not change in the South. The slave population grew to 680,000 in 1790.

Economic

Because of the size of the new country, the United States had the potential to expand westward. It also took a role in trading with the other nations and for the first time broke the mercantilist hold that had been placed on the colonies by Great Britain. The Continental Congress printed money, though there was a large debt still to be paid after the war ended.

THE FORMATION OF A NEW GOVERNMENT

The Articles of Confederation

Before the war was even over, the colonies approved the first official government for the United States of America. It was called the Articles of Confederation. **Sherlock** wants you to take a look at the way this government was organized.

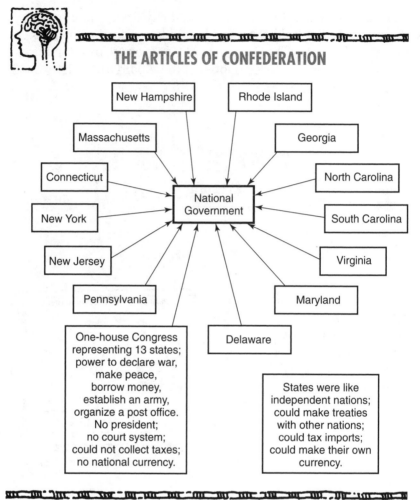

THE ARTICLES OF CONFEDERATION

New Hampshire

Rhode Island

Massachusetts

Georgia

Connecticut

North Carolina

New York

National Government

South Carolina

New Jersey

Virginia

Pennsylvania

Maryland

Delaware

One-house Congress representing 13 states; power to declare war, make peace, borrow money, establish an army, organize a post office. No president; no court system; could not collect taxes; no national currency.

States were like independent nations; could make treaties with other nations; could tax imports; could make their own currency.

Decide why the outer rectangles are all surrounding the center rectangle titled National Government. What does that tell you about the nature of the Articles of Confederation?

Looking at the Articles of Confederation Mind Map, you will notice thirteen rectangles all surrounding one rectangle called the national government. The thirteen rectangles each have a name of the thirteen newly formed states. They have a loose connection to the national government, and when you look at the strengths and weaknesses of the Articles, you should reach the conclusion that the Articles represented a first attempt at organizing the government.

It was a loose relationship because the colonists feared a strong central government and were afraid of a repeat of what they had experienced under England's rule.

HISTORICAL TIDBIT

After the Articles of Confederation were ratified, John Hanson of Maryland was elected president of the one-house Congress. That technically made him the first president of the United States.

The one major accomplishment under the Articles of Confederation was the passage of the Northwest Ordinance in 1787. It created a system of limited government and organized the entire Northwest Territory as a single area. The territory became a new area for eventual westward expansion by the young country.

While the Articles of Confederation was the national form of government, each state also had its own version of government. State constitutions differed, but all emphasized what the Declaration of Independence called "unalienable rights" of life, liberty, and the pursuit of happiness, as well as other rights which would eventually be part of the Bill of Rights; however, because the Articles of Confederation created such a weak central government, many states had conflicts with each other.

The Constitutional Convention

The period between 1781 and 1789 became known as "the critical period" in United States history. Because of the uncertainty and problems created by the Articles of Confederation, the new country struggled to meet its economic obligations. In 1786 a rebellion of farmers, known as Shays' Rebellion, broke out in Massachusetts. Daniel Shays was a farmer who was going to lose his farms because he could not pay his taxes. As a result of his situation, he led other farmers in armed rebellion and marched to the courthouse and armory in Springfield. Shays' army stole weapons and he and his rebels fled to the countryside. Pursued by both New York and Massachusetts militia, he was finally captured in 1787.

The Founding Fathers all came from different parts of the country. Some represented states with large populations; others represented states that had large slave populations. There were also questions raised as to whether the Articles could have just been revised rather than completely changed. Additionally, the delegates also represented different economic interests. Some represented farmers; others represented bankers. All these factors influenced the delegates in the drafting of the new Constitution.

In trying to craft a series of compromises so that a new constitution could be ratified, the delegates argued and debated over three key areas: representation, slavery, and the need for a Bill of Rights to be part of the Constitution.

SHERLOCK CHALLENGE

Take the role of a delegate to the Constitutional Convention and look at the charts that give the differing points of view dealing with these subjects. What compromises would you come up with and how do they compare with the real compromises reached by the delegates?

Constitutional Convention Compromises

Plan A (Favored by large states)	Plan B (Favored by the small states)
Include in the Constitution one House of Representatives based only on population.	Include in the Constitution one house consisting of equal representation.
Plan A (Favored by the North)	**Plan B** (Favored by the South)
Include in the Constitution a provision that bans the importing of slaves and does not count them in the total population of a state.	Include in the Constitution unlimited importing of slaves and count slaves as part of the population.

Therefore, a series of compromises came about. If you look at the major areas of disagreement, you will notice they involve representation and slavery. What compromises were made? The Bill of Rights, another area of contention, is discussed later.

Representation

There were two plans. The New Jersey plan favored a single legislative body based on equal representation of the thirteen states. The Virginia plan favored a single legislative body based on the population of the state; thus larger states would have more representatives than smaller states. The Great Compromise created two houses of Congress: One house, called the House of Representatives, was based on the Virginia Plan; the other house, called the Senate, was based on the New Jersey plan.

Slavery

This was a problem that would not be settled until the Civil War; however, the new Constitution ended slave trade in 1808. The issue of how to count slaves in the newly formed House of Representatives caused a major split. The North did not want slaves to be counted since they did not have any legal rights. The South wanted slaves to be counted to give the South more representation. The compromise reached provided for every five slaves to be counted as three people for the purposes of representation; it was therefore called the "three-fifths compromise."

OLD NORTHWEST
SLAVERY BANNED

ORIGINAL
13 COLONIES

SLAVERY
PERMITTED

OLD
SOUTHWEST

The Constitution

The lines were drawn and two factions emerged to argue for and against the approval of the new Constitution. This process, called *ratification*, needed nine of the thirteen states to vote for the new document. Those who were in favor of the Constitution were called the Federalists. Those who opposed the Constitution were called the Anti-Federalists. One of the Federalist leaders, Alexander Hamilton, argued through the publication of *The Federalist Papers* that there was a need for a strong central government. Thomas Jefferson, leader of the Anti-Federalists, still believed in a loose association of the states.

Sherlock **Question:** Which side would you join, the Federalists or Anti-Federalists?

The Constitution was finally ratified, but not until a series of heated debates took place in each of the states. Look at the chart of the ratification process.

The Ratification of the Constitution

Order	State	Date	Votes for	Votes against
1	Delaware	December 7, 1787	30	0
2	Pennsylvania	December 12, 1787	46	23
3	New Jersey	December 18, 1787	38	0
4	Georgia	January 2, 1788	26	0
5	Connecticut	January 9, 1788	128	40
6	Massachusetts	February 6, 1788	187	168
7	Maryland	April 28, 1788	63	11
8	South Carolina	May 23, 1788	149	73
9	New Hampshire	June 21, 1788	57	47
10	Virginia	June 25, 1788	89	79
11	New York	July 26, 1788	30	27
12	North Carolina	November 21, 1789	194	77
13	Rhode Island	May 29, 1790	34	32

Looking at the ratification chart, it is surprising to see how close the vote was in Massachusetts, New Hampshire,

Virginia, New York, and Rhode Island. Also, since the Constitution needed nine states to ratify, it is interesting

to note that two key states, Virginia and New York, approved it after it had technically been ratified. Nobody knows what would have happened if a big state like New York had voted it down!

In the last part of this chapter, Sherlock will explore the important principles of government established in the Constitution.

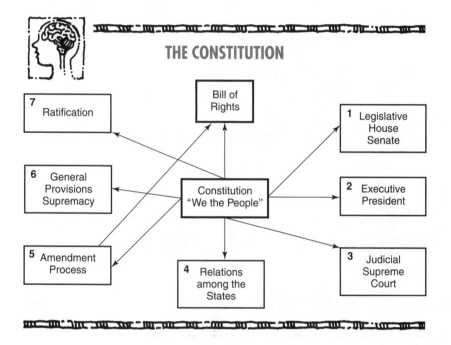

THE CONSTITUTION

| 7 Ratification |
| Bill of Rights |
| 1 Legislative House Senate |
| 6 General Provisions Supremacy |
| Constitution "We the People" |
| 2 Executive President |
| 5 Amendment Process |
| 4 Relations among the States |
| 3 Judicial Supreme Court |

They are:

- **limited government** based on popular sovereignty

Limited government—Through the election of our officials, called popular sovereignty, government can only act with powers given to it by the people.

• separation of powers and checks and balances

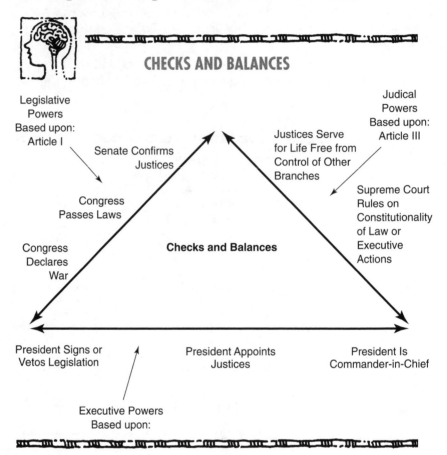

CHECKS AND BALANCES

Legislative
Powers
Based upon:
Article I

Senate Confirms
Justices

Congress
Passes Laws

Congress
Declares
War

Judical
Powers
Based upon:
Article III

Justices Serve
for Life Free from
Control of Other
Branches

Supreme Court
Rules on
Constitutionality
of Law or
Executive
Actions

Checks and Balances

President Signs or
Vetos Legislation

President Appoints
Justices

President Is
Commander-in-Chief

Executive Powers
Based upon:

- **federalism**

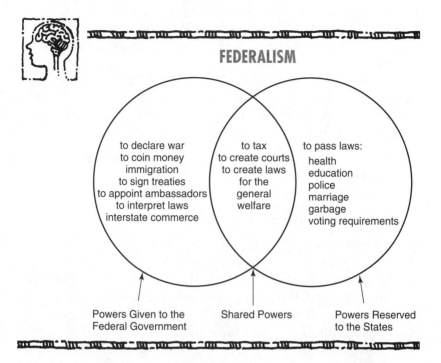

FEDERALISM

to declare war
to coin money
immigration
to sign treaties
to appoint ambassadors
to interpret laws
interstate commerce

to tax
to create courts
to create laws
for the
general
welfare

to pass laws:
health
education
police
marriage
garbage
voting requirements

Powers Given to the
Federal Government

Shared Powers

Powers Reserved
to the States

- the **supremacy of national laws**

National supremacy—Based on a clause in the Constitution, national laws are superior to state laws.

- the guarantee of personal liberties through a **Bill of Rights**

Bill of Rights—The first ten amendments to the Constitution. They guarantee people certain freedoms such as freedom of press, speech, and religion.

Look at the Constitution Mind Map and describe how the Constitution is organized. Then look at the triangle explanation of separation of powers and the circle representation of federalism. How do these features explain how the government works?

After looking at the Constitution Mind Map, the triangle explanation of the separation of powers, and the circle representation of federalism, you should be able to come up with the following conclusions about the Constitution:

- The introduction to the Constitution beginning with the words "We the people" is called the Preamble and it describes the purposes of the Constitution.

The Constitution has seven articles:

- Articles I–III describe the three branches of government—the Legislative body, whose major responsibility is to make the Laws, called Congress, consisting of a House of Representatives and Senate; the Executive branch, run by the president, whose major responsibility is to Enforce the laws; and the Judicial branch, where the power of the courts is described and whose major function is to Judge whether the laws of the Congress and the actions of the president are legal.
- Article IV describes the rules and regulations for the states.
- Article V discusses how the Constitution can be amended; an example of this is the Bill of Rights.
- Article VI states that the Constitution is "the law of the land" and is supreme.
- Article VII describes how the Constitution needed the approval of nine out of the thirteen states to be ratified.

The diagram called the triangle theory describes in detail how each branch of government has specific powers; that is called "separation of powers," and the way those powers guarantee that no one branch becomes too powerful is called "checks and balances."

The diagram called the circle theory illustrates how there is a division of powers between the federal government and state governments, each having unique powers. There are also powers that are shared by the federal and state governments. This is called federalism.

HISTORICAL TIDBIT

One of the debates held at the Constitutional Convention that was put on hold was the question regarding the Bill of Rights. The Anti-Federalists insisted that a Bill of Rights be part of the original Constitution. The Federalists believed there were sufficient guarantees against government abuses in the Constitution. They reached an agreement that led to the ratification of the Bill of Rights two years after the Constitution was ratified.

The Bill of Rights

SHERLOCK CHALLENGE

Look at the summary of the Bill of Rights. Even though there are ten amendments describing our rights, there are twenty-seven individual rights listed. What are those rights?

Though the Bill of Rights consists of ten amendments, in fact, it guarantees many more freedoms:

Amendment I—Religious establishment is prohibited; free exercise of religion; freedom of speech; freedom of the press; the right to petition, and the right to assembly.
Amendment II—The right to keep and bear arms.
Amendment III—Soldiers can only be quartered with the consent of the owner and only in time of war.
Amendment IV—The right of search and seizure is regulated; the right of privacy; search warrants are required with probable cause.

Due Process (the rights of the accused) Amendments:

Amendment V—Provisions concerning prosecution: Indictment is needed; no double jeopardy; life, liberty, or property cannot be taken without due process of law; one can't be made to testify against oneself (self-incrimination).
Amendment VI—The right to a speedy trial is guaranteed; one must be informed of the nature of the

crime; one must be able to confront, call, and question witnesses; one must have the assistance of a lawyer.

Amendment VII—The right to a trial by jury.

Amendment VIII—Excessive bail or fines and cruel punishment are prohibited.

Amendment IX—Rights not listed in the Constitution cannot be taken away.

Amendment X—Reserved power clause giving rights to the states under the Constitution.

The Constitution is much more than an old historic document. It is a living, flexible instrument that provides for the framework of our democracy.

SHERLOCK'S MATCHING MADNESS

Match the name of the law passed by the British to what the law attempted to do to the colonists.

The Sugar Act of 1764	Placed a tax on colonial documents
The Currency Act of 1764	Required colonists to provide British troops with provisions and a home
The Quartering Act of 1765	Enabled the British to seize smugglers and search the ship using a writ of assistance
The Stamp Act of 1765	Imposed a new set of taxes on goods imported from England. Resulted in more British troops in Boston
The Declaratory Act of 1766	Outlawed colonial money
The Townshend Acts of 1777	Established the English Parliament as the sole authority to make all laws binding on the colonies

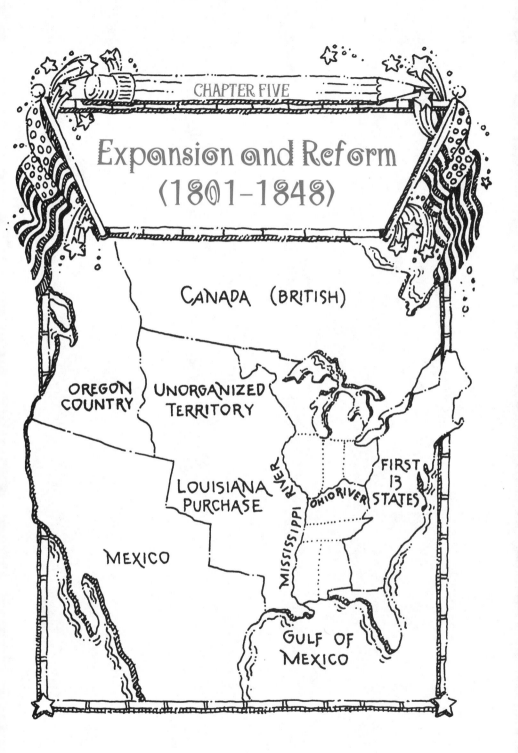

CHAPTER FIVE

Expansion and Reform (1801-1848)

CANADA (BRITISH)

OREGON COUNTRY

UNORGANIZED TERRITORY

LOUISIANA PURCHASE

MISSISSIPPI RIVER

OHIO RIVER

FIRST 13 STATES

MEXICO

GULF OF MEXICO

Tis our true policy to steer clear of permanent Alliances.
—George Washington's Farewell Address, 1796

Time Line (1789–1848)

1789 George Washington elected first president

1789 Washington appoints first cabinet members

1792 Eli Whitney invents the cotton gin

1793 Congress passes Fugitive Slave Act

1794 Whiskey Rebellion against high taxes

1795 Jay Treaty settles issues with Great Britain

1796 John Adams elected president

1798 XYZ Affair

1798 Alien and Sedition Acts passed

1798 Virginia and Kentucky Resolutions passed

1800 Thomas Jefferson elected president

1800 Government moves to Washington, D.C.

1801 John Marshall named Chief Justice of Supreme Court

1803 *Marbury v. Madison* decided by Supreme Court

1803 Louisiana Purchase

1804 Lewis and Clark expedition begins

1804 Hamilton killed by Burr in duel

1807 Robert Fulton invents steamboat

1808 James Madison elected president

1812 War of 1812 begins

1814 Washington, D.C. captured by British

1814 "Star Spangled Banner" written

1814 Treaty of Ghent ends War of 1812

1816 James Monroe elected president

1819 *McCulloch v. Maryland* decided by Supreme Court

1820 Missouri Compromise

1823 Monroe Doctrine

1825 Erie Canal completed

1825 John Quincy Adams elected president by House of Representatives

1828 Andrew Jackson elected president

1831 Trail of Tears

1832 Andrew Jackson reelected

1832 Jackson vetoes chartering of Second National Bank

1832 Nullification crisis

1832 McCormick reaper invented

1836 Martin Van Buren elected president

1840 William Henry Harrison elected president

1841 John Tyler becomes president after Harrison dies in office

1844 James Polk elected president

1846 Mexican War begins

1848 Women's rights convention held in Seneca Falls, New York

1848 Gold discovered in California

1848 Mexican War ends

1848 Zachary Taylor elected president

GROWING PAINS

The newly formed nation created an excitement for the citizens of the young country, but its future destiny faced many obstacles. If not for a combination of outstanding leaders and some good luck, the young republic could have easily been destroyed by enemies from within and from foreign powers.

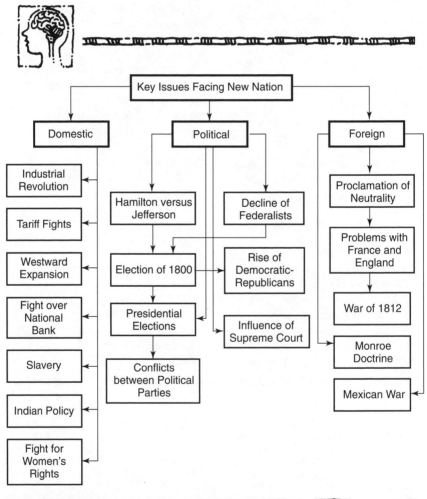

Key Issues Facing New Nation

Domestic
- Industrial Revolution
- Tariff Fights
- Westward Expansion
- Fight over National Bank
- Slavery
- Indian Policy
- Fight for Women's Rights

Political
- Hamilton versus Jefferson
- Decline of Federalists
- Election of 1800
- Rise of Democratic-Republicans
- Presidential Elections
- Influence of Supreme Court
- Conflicts between Political Parties

Foreign
- Proclamation of Neutrality
- Problems with France and England
- War of 1812
- Monroe Doctrine
- Mexican War

Look at the "Key Issues Facing New Nation" Mind Map and the Time Line accompanying this chapter. Imagine that you are a citizen of the United States in the year 1800. Decide what you feel were some of the dangers facing the country. Then decide why the country was able to succeed by listing those areas and events that contributed to its development.

The themes of the time period are outlined by the Mind Map and Time Line. Some of the dangers facing the country were:

- The threats from abroad, ultimately leading to the War of 1812
- Political differences leading to conflicts between parties
- Fights over domestic issues such as tariff policy, the national bank, the Indian policy, and slavery

Some of the factors leading to success include:

- The stand the United States took when Monroe warned Europe to stay out of the Western Hemisphere in his famous Monroe Doctrine
- The expansion of the country westward
- The Industrial Revolution
- Dynamic leadership of presidents such as Jefferson and Jackson

CHAPTER FLASHBACK

If you recall, the last chapter outlined how the nation had a new government called the Articles of Confederation. During what was called the "critical period," people started questioning whether this new government would work. Groups called Federalists and Anti-Federalists argued over the need for a new Constitution. A convention was called in Philadelphia, and after a series of compromises, the Constitution of the United States was ratified in 1789. Two years later the first ten amendments to the Constitution, known as the Bill of Rights, was added to the Constitution.

Our first president

Now the government had to move forward. The newly formed Congress passed the Judiciary Act in 1789, which created the Supreme Court and other federal courts. The House of Repre- sentatives elected the first president of the United States, revolutionary war hero George Washington. One of his first actions was to get the most qualified people involved in the new government. He did this by creating the Cabinet. Since it was not part of the formal Constitution, it became part of what is called the **Unwritten Constitution**.

WASHINGTON

Unwritten Constitution—Those areas of government that are not part of the written Constitution, such as the cabinet and political parties.

Two of Washington's first cabinet appointments were Alexander Hamilton, the leading Federalist who took the position of secretary of the treasury, and Thomas Jefferson, an Anti-Federalist, who was appointed secretary of state.

Look at the following chart. What are the most significant differences between Hamilton and Jefferson? Why do you think Washington appointed these two men who had opposite opinions about most things?

Hamilton	Jefferson
Married into wealth.	Spoke for "the common man."
Believed in a strong central government.	Believed in states' rights.
Favored commerce and industry.	Represented farming interests.
Devised a National Bank.	Felt the Constitution did not allow for the creation of a National Bank.
Wanted a tariff.	Was against a tariff.
Believed in establishing commercial relations with Great Britain.	Supported the French Revolution.

The president's cabinet has become a very important institution of government. When Washington appointed Jefferson and Hamilton, he knew they differed on some important issues such as the role of the federal government and the manner in which the economy should develop. However, he felt that it was essential to have the most able men to serve in the government.

The ultimate success or failure of the new government rested squarely on the shoulders of the new president, George Washington. Besides appointing a cabinet, Washington supported the growth of the country. Immigrants arrived from Europe. Americans were moving westward—New Englanders to Ohio, southerners into Kentucky and Tennessee. The Industrial Revolution also had a positive impact on the country. Eli Whitney invented the cotton gin in 1792, which would eventually transform the southern economy. The Northeast also became more industrialized. Factories laid the groundwork for the newly emerging textile industry and shipping, and commerce became so big that the United States was second only to England in those areas.

Washington's leadership skills also helped the country navigate a safe course. He developed policies for the settlement of territories previously held by Britain and Spain. Three new states were admitted—Vermont (1791), Kentucky (1792), and Tennessee (1796). His advice for the country before he left office after his second term was to "steer clear of permanent alliances." This policy of neutrality became the major characteristic of American foreign policy until the twentieth century.

HISTORICAL TIDBIT

There are over 200 places and things named after George Washington, including a state, our capital, mountains, streams, lakes, counties, colleges, public schools, streets, towns, villages, and monuments.

BIOGRAPHY SPOTLIGHT: GEORGE WASHINGTON

Birthday: February 22, 1732
Birthplace: Wakefield, Virginia
College or University: none
Religion: Episcopalian
Occupation or Profession: Planter, Surveyor, Military
Military Rank: General
Married: (January 6, 1759) Mrs. Martha Dandridge Custis
Children: Two step grandchildren—John "Jackie" Parke Custis and Martha "Patsy" Parke Custis
President Number: First president of the United States
Political Party: Federalist
Runner Up: none
Vice President: John Adams
Age at Inauguration: 57
Served: 1789–1797
Number of terms: Two
Other Offices or Commissions: President of Constitutional Convention, Lieutenant General and Commander in Chief of new United States Army
Died: December 14, 1799
Age at Death: 67
Place of Burial: Mount Vernon, Virginia
Only president to be elected unanimously
Only president inaugurated in two cities—New York and Philadelphia
Only president who did not live in the White House
He was involved in the planning of the Capitol.
There were thirteen stars on the United States flag when Washington became president in 1789.
Five states were added to the Union during Washington's presidency—North Carolina (1789), Rhode Island (1790), Vermont (1791), Kentucky (1792), and Tennesee (1796).

EARLY FOREIGN POLICY CONTROVERSIES

EARLY FOREIGN POLICY CONTROVERSIES

Washington's decision to leave office after two terms began a long-standing tradition that lasted until Franklin Roosevelt decided to run for a third term. John Adams, our second president, was the last Federalist to become president of the United States. Even though the United States had a stated policy of neutrality, the Adams administration was plagued by foreign policy controversies similar to those that took place during Washington's administration. Let's briefly trace them:

Washington's foreign policy incidents

Citizen Genêt Affair (1794)

After Washington broke a treaty with France, its diplomat Edmond Charles Genêt was sent to the United States. Known as Citizen Genêt, he angered the American government when he disagreed with the president. Genêt then personally took his case to the American people and Washington asked France to recall him.

Jay Treaty (1794)

The treaty settled a dispute with Britain but failed to address the issue of the seizure of American ships and the forcing of American sailors into the British navy, known as *impressment*.

Adams's foreign policy incidents

The XYZ Affair (1798)

Three American diplomats, known as X, Y, and Z, reported that the French demanded loans and bribes from American officials. Americans became hostile toward France and, as a result, the United States strengthened its armed forces.

Alien and Sedition Acts (1798)

Because of American hostility toward France, Congress passed these acts that gave the president the power to punish aliens in times of war. They also gave the government the right to arrest people in times of war if they spoke or wrote things against the government.

Kentucky and Virginia Resolution (1798)

In response to the Alien and Sedition Acts, Kentucky and Virginia both passed state laws that they would not enforce these acts in their states. This action was called *nullification,* but this state action was not carried out. Eventually, the idea was used by the South when they seceded from the Union and the Civil War began.

After looking at the early foreign policy controversies, why do you think the government decided to pass the Alien and Sedition Acts? What do you think would happen today if the government supported a law like this?

As you will soon see, threats from England and France posed a real problem for the United States in the early 1800s. The events listed all give you a hint as to why this is so. One thing is certain. As a very young country with a weak military, we were very fortunate that Europe had its own problems. The Alien and Sedition Acts established the idea that in times of national crisis, the government can limit the civil liberties of individuals. Whether you believe this makes sense depends to a certain extent on the nature of the threat posed to the United States.

POLITICAL DEVELOPMENTS AFTER 1800

The election of 1800

The election of 1800 proved to be a turning point in American politics. It was a hotly contested election between the

Federalist party headed by John Adams, and a new party formed by Thomas Jefferson called the Democratic-Republicans. Jefferson won the election and the results signaled the downfall of the Federalist party, though there were still many Federalists in the government. One controversy surrounding the election involved a Supreme Court case called *Marbury v. Madison*. During the last hours of his presidency, John Adams appointed a number of Federalists as judges. They were called "midnight judges." Jefferson did not like these appointments and challenged them after he was elected. Jefferson brought the case before the court under a law establishing the procedures for Supreme Court review. In what is called a landmark decision, the Supreme Court, under new chief justice, John Marshall, for the first time said that the law that established the procedure to appeal a case to a Supreme Court was unconstitutional. This power, called **judicial review**, is one of the most important powers the Supreme Court has.

JEFFERSON

Judicial review—The power of the Supreme Court to judge whether actions of the president, laws of Congress, or laws passed by states are constitutional.

Jefferson faced many problems as president. We will be looking at them as, later in this chapter, we put under the microscope the domestic and foreign policy issues facing the nation. But let's take a closer look at Thomas Jefferson, who many historians have called one of our greatest presidents.

Here is an example of a quote Thomas Jefferson dealing with slavery:

*Nobody wishes more **ardently** [passionately] to see an **abolition** [end of slavery], not only of the trade, but of the condition of slavery; and certainly, nobody will be more willing to **encounter** [meet] every sacrifice for that object.*
— Thomas Jefferson to Brissot de Warville, 1788

Jefferson was against slavery. The irony is that he owned slaves himself and, according to the results of a DNA test conducted in 1998, had an affair with one of them, Sally Hemmings.

Jefferson has been described as a person with "a sense of the extraordinary range of his talents, his insatiable thirst for knowledge, his watchful use of time, and the larger community that lived and worked at Monticello."

 ## HISTORICAL TIDBIT

Thomas Jefferson was the first president to walk to his inauguration. He wore a plain gray suit, and most historians wrote that it was his belief in the common man that made him decide to walk. The truth was that a new $6,000 carriage never arrived because of bad weather.

One of the most important political events of the time was the relocation of the capital in 1800 to what was named Washington, D.C. With the establishment of the District of Columbia as the nation's capital, a new home then had to be built for the Congress. The capital has undergone many changes in its history.

Visiting the Capitol: Public Tours of the Capitol: The following visitation policy is in effect at the Capitol.

The Capitol is open to the public for guided tours only. Tours will be conducted from 9:00 A.M. to 4:30 P.M. Monday through Saturday. (The Capitol is not available for tours on Sundays.) The Capitol will be open on all federal holidays except Thanksgiving Day and Christmas Day.

Visitors must obtain free tickets for tours on a first-come, first-served basis, at the new Capitol Visitors Center.

The Congressional Special Services Office provides information about tours for the disabled by telephone at 202-224-4048 (voice) or 202-224-4049 (TDD). Additional accessibility information is available.

One of the most bitter political rivalries reached a deadly conclusion in 1804. Alexander Hamilton and Aaron Burr had been political opponents. After the election of 1804, their disagreements reached a peak when Burr challenged Hamilton to a duel. Hamilton accepted and was shot to death.

 **HISTORICAL TIDBIT**

There were other famous Americans who also were involved in duels. They included Benedict Arnold, Henry Clay, De Witt Clinton, Andrew Jackson, and Abraham Lincoln.

The duel between Hamilton and Burr was one of the saddest events in American history. After reading the account, you should be able to detect Burr's anger as he uses such charged words as "evasive, not altogether decorous." Then he sets the stage for the duel as he states clearly to Hamilton that "you were ready to meet the consequences."

When you look at political issues, you have to focus on the presidents who were elected to office. Once the presidents were sworn in, each of them made a mark on the nation. One election made history when no candidate received a majority of what is called the electoral votes—the number of votes, based on how many states a candidate wins—needed to win the election. This process is defined in the Constitution and is called the **electoral college.**

Electoral college—The process in which electors determined by the size of each state choose the president after the majority of people in each state vote.

YOU DECIDE:

Let's take a look at the results of the election:

Candidate	Popular Vote	Electoral Vote
Andrew Jackson	153,544	99
John Quincy Adams	108,740	84
William H. Crawford	46,618	41
Henry Clay	47,136	37

Who do you think won the election? If you said Jackson, you are wrong. Since no candidate received a majority of the electoral votes, the House of Representatives decided the outcome and chose Adams.

Each president has what you can call a "claim to fame." **Thomas Jefferson (1801–1809)**—Helped expand the United States through his purchase of the Louisiana Territory from France. Died on July 4

James Madison (1809–1817)—Known as the "Father of the Constitution," he called for a declaration of war in 1812.

James Monroe (1817–1825)—People called his presidency "the era of good feeling." He also issued the Monroe Doctrine.

John Quincy Adams (1825–1829)—Won a disputed election; favored the construction of roads and canals.

Andrew Jackson (1829–1837)—Called "Old Hickory," he also led the fight for the National Bank and supported the removal of Indians from their homes.

Martin Van Buren (1837–1841)—Opposed the expansion of slavery; had to fight an economic depression during his administration.

William Henry Harrison (1841)—Ran for election using a campaign slogan "Tippecanoe [a battle that Harrison won during the war of 1812] and Tyler too"; died in office one month after he was sworn in.

John Tyler (1841–1845)—The first vice-president to become president because of a death of the elected president; a believer in states' rights.

James Polk (1845–1849)—encouraged the expansion of the nation from coast to coast; signed a declaration of war against Mexico in 1848.

Zachary Taylor (1849–1850)—Called "Old Rough and Ready," this career soldier resisted attempts by the South to leave the union; died in office.

DOMESTIC ISSUES FACING THE NATION

There were striking themes that characterized the concerns of the citizens of the young country. They were:

- The creation of the National Bank. Favored by Alexander Hamilton in 1791, it would be the central bank for the United States. It would have the power to lend money and would regulate the country's economy. Many felt the bank's creation was illegal. Those people were called **strict constructionists**.

Strict constructionists—Those who believe the interpretation of the Constitution should not be flexible.

Loose constructionists—Those who believe the interpretation of the Constitution should be flexible.

The people who favored the bank were called **loose constructionists**. A Supreme Court case called *McCulloch v. Maryland* settled the issue. The court ruled that the bank was legal.

- The fight over protective tariffs. The North favored a high protective tariff, a tax on imported goods, in order to get maximum profits on goods it made. The South was against it because it was afraid that its exports would be taxed by other countries.
- The effects of the Industrial Revolution. Inventions such as Eli Whitney's cotton gin and McCormick's reaper ushered in the Industrial Revolution. Its impact was widespread as new forms of transportation, such as the railroad, and new means of transporting goods, such as canals, also appeared.

When New York governor De Witt Clinton supported and received approval to begin construction of the Erie Canal in 1810, little did he know how it would change the face of transportation. Besides bringing the cities of Albany and Buffalo closer together, the canal, when completed, was a model for future transportation. The finished canal was 425 miles long, 40 feet wide, and only 4 feet deep. New boats had to be built that could travel on the canal. The steamboat, invented by Robert Fulton, became one of the first passenger boats to travel on the canal. The impact of the canal on westward expansion was striking: Lumber shipments and grain headed east, new immigrants moved west, and new markets would open up all along the canal. Buffalo's population increased almost tenfold by 1840.

Territorial expansion

Manifest Destiny

The drive toward the West. Also called *manifest destiny*, the belief that it was God's will that the United States expand its boundaries from the East Coast to the West Coast. The Louisiana Purchase engineered by Thomas Jefferson, exploration of uncharted territory by Lewis and Clark, the Mexican War, and eventually the gold rush in California achieved this goal.

SHERLOCK MAP CHALLENGE

To explore how the United States achieved its goal of expanding its borders from coast to coast, look at the following map:

Identify the following land obtained by the United States:

- The thirteen original colonies
- Territory obtained by original colonies
- Land ceded by Spain in 1819
- The Louisiana Purchase in 1803
- Territory gained from the Mexican War 1845
- Land ceded by Mexico 1848
- Gadsen Purchase 1853
- Oregon Territory

EYEWITNESS ACCOUNT: LEWIS AND CLARK EXPEDITION:

The Lewis and Clark expedition gave the United States the first account of the uncharted Louisiana territory. Lewis and Clark kept a diary of their journey. What follows are excerpts from the diary:

May 14, 1804

All the preparations being completed, we left our encampment. This spot is at the mouth of the Wood River, a small stream which empties itsef into the Mississippi, opposite to the entrance of the Missouri . . .

. . . Not being able to set sail before four o'clock P.M., we did not make more than four miles, and encamped on the first island opposite a small creek called Cold Water.

May 24, 1804

Passing near the southern shore, the bank fell in so fast as to oblige us to cross the river instantly, between the northern side and a sandbar which is constantly moving and banking with the violence of the current. The boat struck on it and would have upset immediately, if the men had not jumped into the water and held her, til the sand washed from under her.

Sherlock's Question: How did Lewis and Clark's expedition help the development of the United States?

Slavery

A full discussion of this issue will take place in the next chapter, but legislation such as the **Missouri Compromise** tried to address that issue.

Missouri Compromise—A law passed allowing slavery in Missouri and in new states south of that location and did not allow slavery in new states north of that line.

The Native Americans

As a result of two Supreme Court cases, and the support of President Andrew Jackson, the Indians living in Georgia were sent on a *trail of tears* (see below).

The story of the Trail of Tears is a sad one. After President Jackson signed the Indian Removal Act, the Cherokee nation was ordered to leave Georgia. The Indian people suffered tremendously on their long journey, and 4,000 died during the forced removal.

The suffrage movement

The movement advocating women's rights, culminated with the Seneca Falls Convention in 1848, where women leaders, Susan B. Anthony and Elizabeth Cady Stanton, called *suffragettes*, urged that women be given the right to vote.

 ### Time Line of Early Women's Suffrage

1821—Emma Hart Willard founded the Troy Female Seminary in New York—the first endowed school for girls.

1833—Oberlin College became the first coeducational college in the United States. In 1841, Oberlin awarded the first academic degrees to three women. Early graduates included Lucy Stone and Antoinette Brown.

1836—Sarah Grimké began her speaking career as an abolitionist and a women's rights advocate. She was eventually silenced by male abolitionists who considered her public speaking a liability.

1837—The first National Female Anti-Slavery Society convention met in New York City. Eighty-one delegates from twelve states attended.

1837—Mary Lyon founded Mount Holyoke College in Massachusetts, eventually the first four-year college exclusively for women in the United States. Mt. Holyoke was followed by Vassar in 1861 and Wellesley and Smith Colleges, both in 1875. In 1873, the School Sisters of Notre Dame founded a school in Baltimore, Maryland, which eventually became the nation's first college for Catholic women.

1839—Mississippi passed the first Married Woman's Property Act.

1844—Female textile workers in Massachusetts organized the Lowell Female Labor Reform Association (LFLRA) and demanded a ten-hour workday. This was one of the first permanent labor associations for working women in the United States.

1848—The first women's rights convention in the United States was held in Seneca Falls, New York. Many participants signed a "Declaration of Sentiments and Resolutions" that outlined the main issues and goals for the emerging women's movement. Thereafter, women's rights meetings were held on a regular basis.

Pick out what you think is an event that helped the movement and an event that hurt the movement. Then look at the Declaration of Rights and Sentiments, the document voted on at the Seneca Falls convention.

SHERLOCK DOCUMENT CHALLENGE:

The Declaration of Rights and Sentiments:

"When, in the course of human events, it becomes necessary for one portion of the family of man to assume among the people of the earth a position different from that which they have hitherto occupied, but one to which the laws of nature and of nature's God entitle them, a decent respect to the opinions of mankind requires that they should declare the causes that impel them to such a absolution.

We hold these truths to be self-evident: that all men and women are created equal; that they are endowed by their Creator with certain inalienable rights; that among these are life, liberty, and the pursuit of happiness; that to secure these rights governments are instituted, deriving their just powers from the consent of the governed. Whenever any form of government becomes destructive of these ends, it is the right of those who suffer from it to refuse allegiance to it, and to insist upon the institution of a new government, laying its foundation on such principles, and organizing its powers in such form, as to them shall seem most likely to effect their safety and happiness.

Sherlock's Questions: What other document does this remind you of? What do you think was the purpose of this document?

The fight for the women's right to vote did not end until the passage of the Nineteenth Amendment in 1920, but leaders of the movement were pushing for that right even in the 1800s. When you look at the Library of Congress Time Line of events, it becomes obvious that the fight was going to be a long one. The first turning point came in 1848 in Seneca Falls, New York. The convention passed the Declaration of Rights and Sentiments. Even looking at the opening section, you should be able to see a similarity between that document and the Declaration of Independence.

FOREIGN POLICY DEVELOPMENTS

The final section of this chapter deals with the development of United States foreign policy from 1800 to 1850. Washington's famous Proclamation of Neutrality charted the course of foreign policy for the country. The country had to react to external forces, especially the threats from Europe. Along with this policy, as we have seen, the country also pursued a policy of manifest destiny. To achieve this goal, the nation's leaders sometimes had to modify the policy of neutrality.

HISTORICAL TIDBIT

Before burning Washington, D.C., the British occupied the House of Representatives and took a mock vote on whether or not to destroy the nation's capital. There was no doubt about the outcome of this vote.

The War of 1812 was one of the most dangerous wars America ever fought. Coming so close after the American Revolution, it gave England the chance to regain its lost territory. Fortunately for the United States, however, the country was able to fight England to a draw. Two of the key events are the American victory led by Andrew Jackson at the Battle of New

Orleans and the successful burning of Washington, D.C., by the British. This war was the only time in American history that a country was able to attack the internal borders of the United States. The account of the attack on Fort McKinley and the writing of "The Star Spangled Banner" by Francis Scott Key gives you an idea of the emotions stirred by this war.

The War of 1812

This war was fought to establish respect for the United States. Even though we were not prepared to go to war, President Madison signed a declaration of war. Those in favor of the war, called "war hawks," cheered the decision. Some of the battles that took place came very close to reversing the gains the young country had made since it became independent.

The Monroe Doctrine

In 1823 President Monroe realized that Europe posed a threat to their former colonies in Latin America. Through a brilliant move, the issuance of the Monroe Doctrine, Europe was put on notice that North and South America would no longer be "subjects for future colonization." This doctrine established the future policy the United States would follow in Latin America. It also warned Russia that it had no right to pursue areas near Alaska.

The Mexican War

A good example of how manifest destiny caused the United States to move away from Washington's Proclamation of Neutrality was the Mexican War. The treaty with Mexico achieved the goal of getting a large chunk of territory including California, Nevada, Utah, Arizona, New Mexico, Texas, and parts of Colorado and Wyoming, all for the sum of $15 million.

 HISTORICAL TIDBIT

After winning the Mexican War, President Taylor ordered William Sherman to explore the newly acquired territory. After he returned, Sherman reported to the president that he believed the land was so useless that the United States should go back to war against Mexico in order to return the land!

Another war that was completely different from the War of 1812 was the Mexican War. This war was fought to gain more territory and achieve the goals of manifest destiny. You will see that it was a relatively easy victory. The result was the acquisition of a large land area, now known as Texas and New Mexico.

 SHERLOCK'S MATCHING MADNESS:

Match the president with his accomplishment.

Thomas Jefferson	Led the fight for the National Bank
James Madison	Ran for election using the slogan "Tippecanoe and Tyler, too"
John Quincy Adams	Signed a declaration of war against Mexico
Andrew Jackson	Called "old rough and ready"
Martin Van Buren	Helped expand the United States as a result of the Louisiana Purchase
William Henry Harrison	Known as "Father of the Constitution"
John Tyler	His presidency was known as "the era of good feeling"
James Polk	Had to fight an economic depression
Zachary Taylor	First vice-president to become president because of a death of the elected president

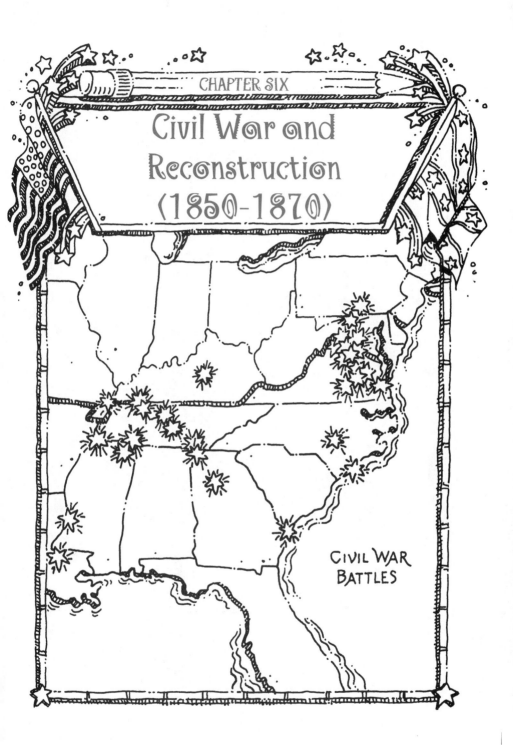

CHAPTER SIX

Civil War and Reconstruction (1850-1870)

CIVIL WAR BATTLES

A house divided against itself cannot stand. I believe this government cannot endure permanently half-slave and half-free.

—Abraham Lincoln, 1858

Time Line (1820–1870)

1820 Missouri Compromise

1831 *The Liberator* published by William Lloyd Garrison

1837 Frederick Douglass, fugitive slave, given freedom

1841 Supreme Court rules in favor of *Amistad* slaves

1850 Compromise of 1850

1852 Harriet Beecher Stowe publishes *Uncle Tom's Cabin*

1854 Kansas-Nebraska Act

1857 Bloody Kansas

1857 Dred Scott Decision

1858 Lincoln-Douglas debates

1860 Abraham Lincoln elected president

1861 Kansas enters the Union as a free state

1861 Southern states, eventually numbering 11, form Confederacy

1861 Civil War begins with Confederate attack on Fort Sumter, South Carolina

1863 Lincoln issues Emancipation Proclamation, freeing slaves

1863 Battle of Gettysburg halts Lee's drive north, the decisive turning point of Civil War

1864 General William Tecumseh Sherman captures and burns Atlanta; captures Savannah

1865 Thirteenth Amendment ratified

1865 Lee surrenders at Appomattox Court House, Virginia

1865 Lincoln assassinated

1865 Johnson begins Reconstruction

1866 Fourteenth Amendment ratified

1868 Impeachment and acquittal of Andrew Johnson

1868 Ulysses S. Grant elected president

1870 Fifteenth Amendment ratified

CAUSES OF THE CIVIL WAR

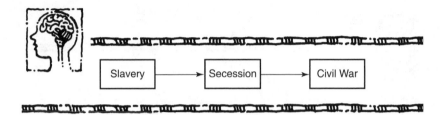

Slavery ——→ Secession ——→ Civil War

The state of America in the 1850s could be described as having a dual character—half-slave and half-free. **Sectionalism** was a main feature of the country's makeup.

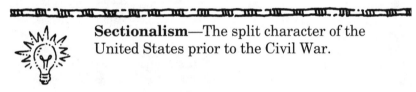

Sectionalism—The split character of the United States prior to the Civil War.

Even foreign visitors like Alexis de Tocqueville, a Frenchman who wrote *Democracy in America*, observed the terrible split in the United States between the rich and poor, the North and the South, the free and those in slavery.

The physical geography of the United States in 1850 was characteristic of a nation that had more than twenty-one million people living in thirty-one states. The eastern part of the country had industry; the Midwest and South were agricultural. In 1849 gold was discovered in California and the rush was on! Typical of the industrial East were textiles, lumber, clothing, machinery, leather, and woolen goods. Shipping also reached its height of activity. The South based its economy on agriculture, specifically growing tobacco and, most important, cotton. The Midwest began to produce goods for the rest of the country. Inventions such as Eli Whitney's cotton gin and the McCormick reaper increased the capability of farm production.

Slavery was the issue that split the country down the middle. The South resented the North's large profits made from marketing the South's cotton crop. Slavery, described by those who were "politically correct," was called the *peculiar institution*. As we discussed in previous chapters, sectional lines had been drawn based on the question of slavery. By 1850 the South did not feel responsible for the institution of slavery since it had been a way of life for over 200 years.

Slave Statistics (1860)
Minority of whites held slaves.
46,274 planters owned at least 20 slaves.
More than half of the slaves worked on plantations.
"Poor southern whites" did not own slaves.

The fact remained that northern hatred of slavery was to a large extent due to the treatment of the slaves by their owners.

SHERLOCK'S EYEWITNESS ACCOUNT:

Look at the following eyewitness account. What was Douglass's point of view about why slaves were whipped? Pick out the words that give you a hint.

A mere look, word, or motion—a mistake, accident, or want of power—are all matters for which a slave may be whipped at any time. Does a slave look dissatisfied? It is said, he has the devil in him, and it must be whipped out. Does he forget to pull off his hat at the approach of a white person? Then he is wanting in reverence, and should be whipped for it.

Source: *Narrative of the Life of Frederick Douglass, An American Slave* (3rd English ed., Leeds, 1846)

After reading the account by Frederick Douglass, the first fugitive slave to be given his freedom, you can see how easy it was for a slave to be whipped. The slightest fault was an excuse for a slave to be punished. Look for the questions that Douglass raises as a clue to the reasons why slaves were treated so brutally.

Uncle Tom's Cabin was one of the most dramatic fictional accounts ever written about slavery. In fact, many historians point to it as a cause of the Civil War. The character Jim Crow was also introduced in the book. The name was later used to describe laws that were passed in the South that kept the freed slaves separated from whites.

The catalyst for war

After defeating Mexico in 1847, the United States increased its size by gaining what is now Arizona, Nevada, California, Utah, and parts of New Mexico, Colorado, and Wyoming. With the discovery of gold in California, new settlers began moving west. The key question: Should slavery be extended into the new territories? The answer to the question came in the form of two pieces of legislation:

The Compromise of 1850

Compromise of 1850—Strict enforcement of Fugitive Slave Act, requiring the return of runaway slaves. California was admitted as a free state. In the new southwest territories, the people were given the right to choose (popular sovereignty).

The Kansas-Nebraska Act in 1854

Kansas-Nebraska Act (1854)—Gave people the right to choose whether the new territories were to be free or slave, even though land was located north of the Missouri Compromise; resulted in Bloody Kansas, armed clashes between northerners and southerners in Kansas.

These events preceded one of the most important and shameful but significant Supreme Court decisions, *Dred Scott v. Sanford*. Scott was a slave who had been brought to free territory and then returned by his master to slave territory. With the aid of his owners, he appealed to the courts for his freedom. In 1857 the Supreme Court, dominated by southerners, in an opinion written by Chief Justice Roger Taney declared that Scott was not a citizen and could not argue for his freedom. The most controversial aspect of the decision was that the court declared that slaves were property. The North now knew that the question of slavery could not be settled legally.

Prior to Lincoln's election, other disturbing sectional events signaled the inevitability of civil war. In 1859 John Brown, led a failed raid on a federal arsenal at Harper's Ferry. His goal was to use the weapons seized and begin a slave revolt. Colonel Robert E. Lee, the soon-to-be leader of the Confederate army, captured Brown after two days of fighting. He was hanged after being convicted for conspiracy and treason. Brown's own words illustrate his intense hatred of the institution.

SHERLOCK'S EYEWITNESS ACCOUNT:

Look at the following eyewitness account. What would you do if you were John Brown?

> . . . *I believe to have interferred as I have done, . . . in behalf of His despised poor, was not wrong, but right. Now, if it be deemed necessary that I should forfeit my life for the furtherance of the ends of*

justice, and mingle my blood further with the blood of my children, and with the blood of millions in this slave country whose rights are disregarded by wicked, cruel and unjust enactments, so let it be done.

Source: Transcript from the trial of John Brown, November 2, 1859

John Brown's raid on Harper's Ferry proved to be a catalyst for war. He was arrested, tried, and hanged. When you look at the diary entry, you will see the agony that Brown went through. It is not surprising that he decided to lead the attack. You must take his passion into account in deciding what you would have done if you were John Brown.

HISTORICAL TIDBIT

John Wilkes Booth, Abraham Lincoln's assassin, was one of the soldiers present when John Brown was hanged.

The South secedes

Events began moving fast. A new politician entered the scene—Abraham Lincoln. In 1858 he opposed Stephen A. Douglas (the key sponsor of the Kansas-Nebraska Act) for election to the U.S. Senate from Illinois. In a series of historic debates, Lincoln reinforced one of his central campaign themes, "A house divided against itself cannot stand." By the end of the seventh debate, Lincoln had become a national figure. Even though he lost the election, it was apparent that the country would soon get to know the man from Illinois.

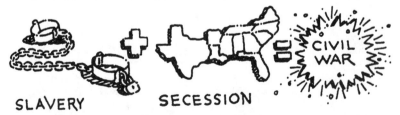

SLAVERY   SECESSION   CIVIL WAR

The rematch between Lincoln and Douglas, this time for president of the United States, split the Democratic party as well as the nation. While Lincoln ran as a Republican, the Southern Democrats nominated John C. Breckenridge as their candidate. This split ensured Lincoln's election. The party positions were clear. Lincoln pledged to keep the union together. His party also pledged a higher tariff, another stand that made the South furious. Douglas and Breckenridge differed on key issues. Lincoln won an easy electoral victory, but had only a plurality of the popular votes.

The South Secedes—
Following is the order in which states
seceded from the Union:

1. South Carolina	5. Georgia	9. Arkansas
2. Mississippi	6. Louisiana	10. North Carolina
3. Florida	7. Texas	11. Tennessee
4. Alabama	8. Virginia	

Look at the following Mind Map and decide who has the greater advantage, the North or the South?

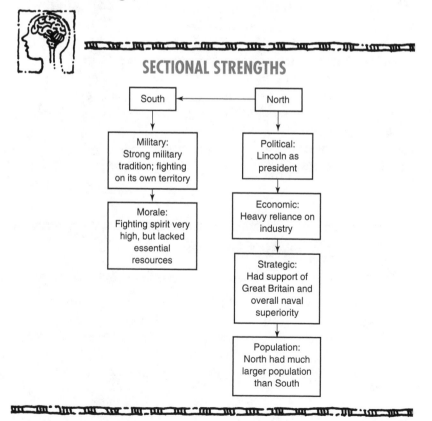

SECTIONAL STRENGTHS

South ← North

South:
Military: Strong military tradition; fighting on its own territory

Morale: Fighting spirit very high, but lacked essential resources

North:
Political: Lincoln as president

Economic: Heavy reliance on industry

Strategic: Had support of Great Britain and overall naval superiority

Population: North had much larger population than South

Relatively speaking, it would appear that both sides had significant advantages. The North certainly had a population, supply, and resource advantage. The South could rely on the fact that most of the fighting was taking place on its home territory. In addition, the South started the war and the people were enthusiastic over the cause. Both sides had some talented generals, though many believed that Robert E. Lee had the edge over any northern military leader.

THE WAR BEGINS

After Lincoln's election, the South did not even wait for his inauguration before the process of secession began. Starting with South Carolina, seven more states quickly declared their independence from the Union. On March 4, 1861, Lincoln was sworn in as president and quickly declared that the act of secession was illegal, calling it "legally void." A month after he became president, Lincoln refused to give up Fort Sumter in South Carolina and the war began.

LINCOLN

HISTORICAL TIDBITS

Some interesting Civil War facts include:

- West Virginia seceded from Virginia to fight on the side of the Union during the Civil War.
- Contrary to popular belief, the Battle of Antietam was the bloodiest battle of the Civil War. The Union had over 12,000 casualties; the South had over 10,000.

- The first African-American to win the Congressional Medal of Honor was Sergeant William H. Carney, who led his unit at the Battle of Charleston.
- Confederate general Stonewall Jackson was wounded in battle by one of his own men at the Battle of Chancellorsville.

What pressures did Lincoln face as president?

If you fully explore the biography of Abraham Lincoln, you will find him to be a complex individual. He never really wanted to engage in a fighting war with the South and always believed that the South should have remained in the Union and try to work out its differences with the North. Once the southern states seceded, Lincoln had one goal in mind—to reunite the country. Though Lincoln was opposed to slavery, if the South had not seceded, it was doubtful whether Lincoln would have led the forces to abolish slavery. Even with the Emancipation Proclamation, Lincoln, by freeing only the slaves in the Confederacy, was careful not to upset the border states that still allowed slavery. Thus, the pressures Lincoln must have felt were tremendous.

The battle lines

The fight to keep the Union together was marked by major battles.

Battles of 1861–1862

1. First Manassas (Bull Run)
2. Forts Henry and Donelson
3. Shiloh (Pittsburg's Landing)
4. Shenandoah Valley
5. Seven Days
6. Second Manassas (Bull Run)
7. Antietam (Sharpsburg)
8. Fredericksburg
9. Murphreesboro (Stone's River)

Battles of 1863

1. Chancellorsville
2. Gettysburg
3. Vicksburg
4. Chickamauga
5. Chattanooga

Battles of 1864–1865

1. Atlanta
2. Wilderness
3. Spotsylvania Courthouse
4. Cold Harbor
5. Sherman's March
6. Franklin
7. Petersburg
8. Nashville
9. Appomattox Campaign

As the bloodiest war in U.S. history, with over 600,000 deaths, the Civil War was marked by battles that sometimes saw cousin fighting cousin. Exploring each individual battle and looking at the battle scenes taken by photographer Matthew Brady, it becomes obvious that this war was one of the most difficult wars the United States ever fought—for both sides. The casualties were extremely heavy. In just a few hours at the Battle of Cold Harbor in Virginia, Grant lost over 12,000 men. In Gettysburg, over 4,000 of Lee's men died, and over 24,000 of his troops were wounded or missing. General Sherman in his "march to the sea" in Georgia destroyed the countryside.

As the North became dominant and began to win battle after battle, Lincoln had to struggle with two major decisions: Should he free the slaves? What kind of plan should he develop to bring the nation back together after the war ended?

SHERLOCK ROLE PLAYING

You are now the president—what would you do about the issues of slavery and unification of the nation?

Look at the opening of the Emancipation Proclamation and pick out the key words and phrases that will tell you how and why Lincoln wanted to free the slaves and what his vision was for the Union.

DOCUMENT CHALLENGE: THE EMANCIPATION PROCLAMATION:

That on the first day of January, in the year of our Lord one thousand eight hundred and sixty-three, all persons held as slaves within any State or designated part of a State, the people whereof shall then be in rebellion against the United States, shall be then, thenceforward, and forever free; and the Executive Government of the United States, including the military and naval authority thereof, will recognize and maintain the freedom of such persons, and will do no act or acts to repress such persons, or any of them, in any efforts they may make for their actual freedom.

The Emancipation Proclamation gives you the evidence you need to answer the question about Lincoln's attitude toward slavery and unification. Without a doubt, the proclamation gave the North a psychological lift. In the South, many slaves fled from their owners. The document itself emphasizes two issues: the freeing of the slaves in the South, and the eventual reunification of the country.

The Emancipation Proclamation

On January 1, 1863, President Abraham Lincoln issued the **Emancipation Proclamation**.

Emancipation Proclamation—Document issued by President Lincoln that freed the slaves ONLY in the states that left the Union. The proclamation did not address the issue of the legality of slaves in the North. That issue was decided by the Thirteenth Amendment to the Constitution passed in 1865.

The proclamation did not address the issue of slavery in the North. Lincoln was afraid of the reaction of the border states where slavery was still legal.

The generals

The two dominant generals fighting the Civil War were Union general Ulysses S. Grant and Confederate general Robert E. Lee. Both were West Point graduates, and each led their respective forces to battle.

If you look at the photos of the two most famous generals of the Civil War, you can get a sense of the pride each had. Both were West Point graduates and they both had a love for their country. Lee made the difficult decision to become the head of the southern forces and waged a brave battle. At the final moment, when he surrendered at the Appomattox Court House, he had to be feeling a sense of sadness at his failure to win the war.

GENERAL LEE

The end of the war

The largest battle of the Civil War took place in the small Pennsylvania town of Gettysburg. It was a momentous battle, with the Confederates making a heroic effort to turn back the Union forces. The casualties were heavy: Over 3,000 Union soldiers and almost 4,000 Confederate soldiers died, and there were more than 20,000 wounded and missing. In one of the most memorable speeches ever given,

President Lincoln addressed a crowd in a dedication of the new national cemetery at Gettysburg.

DOCUMENT CHALLENGE: THE GETTYSBURG ADDRESS:

Four score and seven years ago our fathers brought forth on this continent a new nation, conceived in liberty and dedicated to the proposition that all men are created equal. Now we are engaged in a great civil war, testing whether that nation or any nation so conceived and so dedicated can long endure. We are met on a great battlefield of that war. We have come to dedicate a portion of that field as a final resting-place for those who here gave their lives that the nation might live. It is altogether fitting and proper that we should do this. But in a larger sense, we cannot dedicate, we cannot consecrate, we cannot hallow this ground. The brave men, living and dead, who struggled here have consecrated it far above our poor power to add or detract. The world will little note nor long remember what we say here, but it can never forget what they did here. It is for us the living rather to be dedicated here to the unfinished work which they who fought here have thus far so nobly advanced. It is rather for us to be here dedicated to the great task remaining before us—that from these honored dead we take increased devotion to that cause for which they gave the last full measure of devotion—that we here highly resolve that these dead shall not have died in vain, that this nation under God shall have a new birth of freedom, and that government of the people, by the people, for the people shall not perish from the earth.

Read the speech aloud. Then write down your feelings about what Lincoln was trying to accomplish by giving the speech.

Read the speech aloud more than once. Try to get the feeling of what it must have been like speaking after one of the bloodiest battles of the Civil War. The poetic language Lincoln used, especially the famous conclusion, echoes his vision for the future of the nation.

Lincoln's re-election

In 1864 Lincoln fired General McClellan after the Union
loss at Antietam. Lincoln was then elected to a second term
as president of the United States. In a dramatic moment
during his inauguration he closed his speech with the words
that follow:

> With **malice** toward none; with **charity** for all; with
> **firmness** in the **right**, as God gives us to see the **right**,
> let us strive on to **finish** the work we are in; to bind up
> the nation's wounds; to care for him who shall have borne
> the **battle**, and for his widow and his orphan . . . to do
> all which may **achieve** and **cherish** a **just** and **lasting**
> **peace** among ourselves and with all nations.

Look up any of the words in bold that you don't know and
decide why Lincoln used those words on the occasion of his
inauguration.

As memorable as the Gettysburg Address were the words
Lincoln chose at his second inauguration. Even though the
war was not over, it was obvious that Lincoln was trying to
lay the groundwork for the healing of the nation. He never
believed in punishing the South and the speech reinforced
that message. Just by reading the highlighted words, you can
get an image of what Lincoln was trying to accomplish.

Lincoln's assassination

Within a month after President Lincoln was inaugurated, he
attended the play *Our American Cousin* at Ford's Theatre in
Washington, D.C. An angry Confederate soldier, John Wilkes
Booth, shot the president as he was sitting with Mrs. Lincoln
in the presidential box.

Read the following dream Lincoln had ten days before
he was shot; then write down any dreams you have had that
came true.

Lincoln died the morning after he was shot in the
presidential box at Ford's Theatre watching the play *Our
American Cousin*. In one of the most bizarre historical
stories, Lincoln related the following premonition about an
assassination to his wife and friends:

*I could not have been long in bed when I fell into a
slumber, for I was weary. I soon began to dream. There
seemed to be a death-like stillness about me. Then I heard
subdued sobs, as if a number of people were weeping. I
thought I left my bed and wandered downstairs. I went
from room to room; no living person was in sight, but
the same mournful sounds of distress met me as I passed
along. Where were all the people who were grieving as if
their hearts would break? I was puzzled and alarmed.
What could be the meaning of all this? I kept on until I
arrived at the East Room, which I entered. There I met
with a sickening surprise. Before me was a catafalque,
on which rested a corpse wrapped in funeral vestments.
Around it were stationed soldiers who were acting
as guards; and there was a throng of people, gazing
mournfully upon the corpse, whose face was covered,
others weeping pitifully. "Who is dead in the White
House?" I demanded of one of the soldiers, "The President,"
was his answer; "he was killed by an assassin." I slept no
more that night; and although it was only a dream, I have
been strangely annoyed by it ever since.*

Dreams are very personal. If you are keeping a journal, write
down a dream you remember, then see if it comes true. Most
likely your dreams do not come true, but it is one of those
historical oddities that Lincoln told his wife about this dream.

The job of ending the war and uniting the country was
thrust upon Lincoln's vice-president, Andrew Johnson.
Johnson, a southerner who had remained loyal to the Union
after the war began, was selected by Lincoln as a signal
that his primary goal was to reunite the country after the
war ended. The end came at Appomattox Courthouse in
1865 where Lee surrendered to Grant. Even before the
peace, there were strong hints that the process known as
Reconstruction would be a difficult one.

Reconstruction—The plan and terms adopted
by Congress at the end of the Civil War to bring
the southern states back into the Union.

RECONSTRUCTION

The competing plans of Andrew Johnson and Congress eventually led to the **impeachment** of the president.

 Impeachment—The process that is used to place on trial the president and other government officials. It is defined in the Constitution as "high crimes and misdemeanors."

Even though Johnson was impeached, the Senate and the **Radical Republicans** who supported Johnson's conviction failed to convict him by only one vote and he was able to finish his term of office.

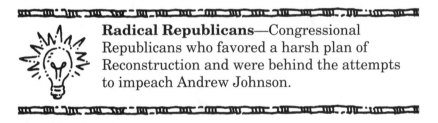 **Radical Republicans**—Congressional Republicans who favored a harsh plan of Reconstruction and were behind the attempts to impeach Andrew Johnson.

Look at the following outline of Reconstruction:

Reconstruction

I. Issues
   A. Civil Rights of Black Citizens
   B. Treatment of Ex-Confederate Soldiers
   C. Readmission of former Confederate states
II. Goals of Reconstruction
   A. Lincoln wanted a plan that would not punish the South
   B. Many northern politicians wanted to protect the slaves
   C. Johnson favored a plan similar to Lincoln's
   D. Congress wanted to control the plan and the Radical Republicans believed that the South should be treated harshly.

III. Results of Reconstruction
   A. Passage of Freedman's Bureau
   B. Adoption of the Thirteenth, Fourteenth, and Fifteenth Amendments to the Constitution.
   C. Military Reconstruction Act
   D. Carpetbaggers and Scalawags
   E. General Amnesty for the South
   F. Passage of Jim Crow Laws and Black Codes

Draw a Mind Map that illustrates the outline. Then write a short paragraph answering: "What was Reconstruction?"

In devising your own Mind Map, you must understand the definitions of Reconstruction terms, then you should build from the outline a series of boxes that contain each of the major Roman numeral issues. From those boxes, you should draw more specific boxes from the capital letter examples. A Reconstruction Mind Map is on page 126.

Reconstruction terms that will help you write an essay:

Freedman's Bureau—Government agency that provided civil rights services for the freed slaves.

Military Reconstruction Act—Formal law establishing military districts for the South during Reconstruction.

Thirteenth, Fourteenth, and Fifteenth Amendments

Thirteenth—Freed the slaves.

Fourteenth—Made the freed slaves citizens and gave them all rights guaranteed to citizens.

Fifteenth—Gave freed slaves the right to vote.

Carpetbagger—Name given by the South to northerners who came to the South after the Civil War with bag in hand and took advantage of the freed slaves.

Scalawags—Negative name given to southerners who cooperated with the Reconstruction plans of the Radical Republicans.

Jim Crow Laws—Laws passed by southern states that discriminated against the freed slaves and created separate facilities for blacks and whites.

Black Codes—Practices established by the South after the Civil War to restrict the freedom of blacks.

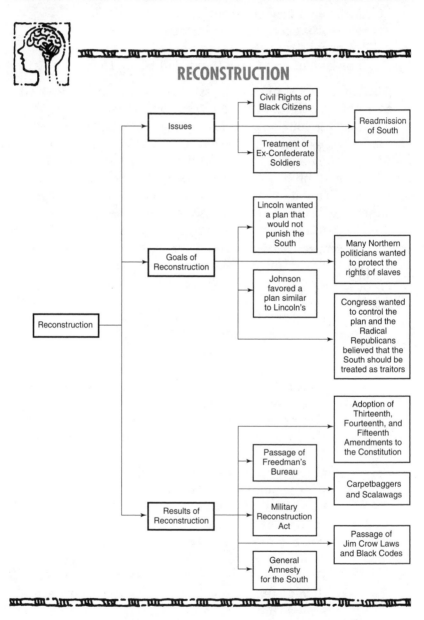

RECONSTRUCTION

A FINAL WORD ABOUT THE CIVIL WAR AND RECONSTRUCTION

Perhaps the most turbulent time in American history, the Civil War and its aftermath, known as Reconstruction, completed the first cycle of America's existence. The Constitution was tested, and it survived. A great president was elected to ensure the peace, and he died a violent death. The nation attempted to reunite, giving its freed citizens equal protection under the law, but the South was able to create a society that they called "separate but equal," their politically correct term for segregation. Technically, the era of Reconstruction ended in 1872 when Congress passed the Amnesty Act, which restored full political rights to former Confederate officials. In the next chapter, we will look more closely at the presidency of Ulysses S. Grant, who guided the nation during this difficult period.

SHERLOCK MATCHING MADNESS:

Match the Civil War term with its meaning.

Freedman's Bureau	Aimed at freed slaves that resulted in segregation for African-Americans
Military Reconstruction Act	Aimed at controlling the civil rights of the freed slaves in the South
Thirteenth Amendment	Gave freed slaves citizenship
Fourteenth Amendment	Freed the slaves
Fifteenth Amendment	Gave freed slaves the right to vote
Carpetbagger	Provided protection for the freed slaves
Scalawag	Established military districts in the South following the Civil War

Jim Crow Laws	Northerners who came to the South after the Civil War and took advantage of the freed slaves
Black Codes	Southerners who were given positions in the government after the Civil War

CHAPTER SEVEN

The Industrial Development of the United States (1868-1898)

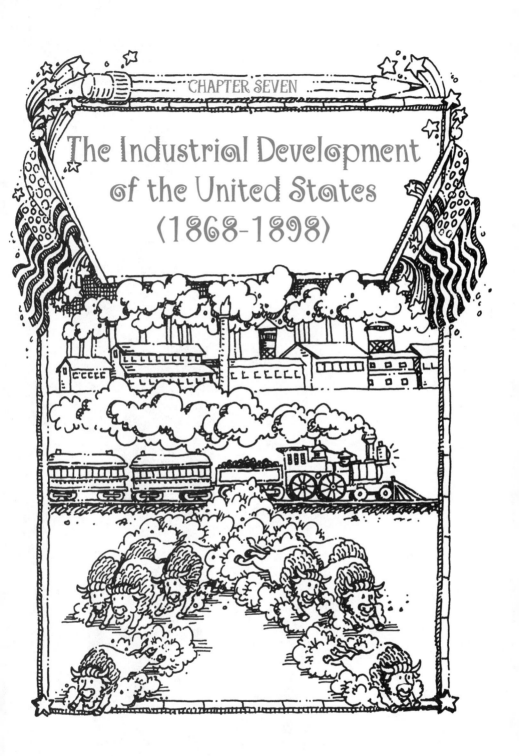

Give me your tired, your poor, your huddled masses yearning to breathe free.
—Emma Lazarus, *The New Colossus*, inscription for the Statue of Liberty

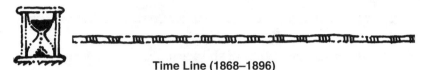

Time Line (1868–1896)

1868 Ulysses S. Grant elected president	**1885** Washington Monument dedicated
1869 Elizabeth Cady Stanton elected president of National Woman Suffrage Association	**1886** Haymarket Square Riot
	1886 American Federation of Labor founded
1869 Transcontinental Railroad completed at Promontory Point, Utah	**1886** Statue of Liberty completed
	1888 William Henry Harrison elected president
1870 Fifteenth Amendment ratified	
1871 First black members of Congress elected	**1890** Frontier closed
	1890 Wounded Knee massacre
1872 Grant reelected	**1890** Sherman Antitrust Act passed
1874 Women's Christian Temperance Union formed	**1892** Homestead strike
	1892 Cleveland defeats Harrison
1876 Rutherford B. Hayes elected president	**1892** Ellis Island named official receiving station for immigrants
1876 Bell invents telephone	
1876 Battle of Little Big Horn	**1894** Pullman strike and general railway strike
1877 Reconstruction officially ends	**1896** *Plessy v. Ferguson* establishes separate but equal doctrine
1879 Edison invents electric lamp	
1880 James A. Garfield elected president	**1896** William McKinley elected president
1881 Garfield assassinated; Chester A. Arthur becomes new president	**1896** Large influx of eastern and southern European immigrants
1881 Standard Oil creates first trust	**1896** McKinley reelected
1884 Grover Cleveland elected president	

THE RISE OF INDUSTRY

Now that the country was back on its feet, a new era of industrial development began. Historians have given it the name **The Gilded Age**.

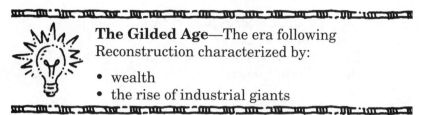

The Gilded Age—The era following Reconstruction characterized by:

- wealth
- the rise of industrial giants

Its impact on all segments of the nation was significant. New industrial leaders, called **captains of industry**, gave birth to large corporations.

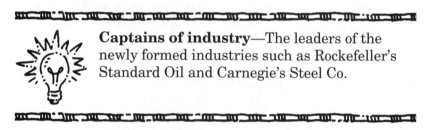
Captains of industry—The leaders of the newly formed industries such as Rockefeller's Standard Oil and Carnegie's Steel Co.

Some people called these new industrial giants **robber barons**.

Robber barons—Negative name for those captains of industry who used their wealth to hurt the poor or to destroy smaller competitors.

There arose a need for labor to support these new factories. Laborers began to organize, and labor unions were formed. Cheap labor was needed to help build the railroads used to transport the goods made by the new industries and the farm products grown. Where was the labor from? From immigrants. The most dramatic period of immigration took place during this time period, but with this immigration, came a negative reaction from **nativists**.

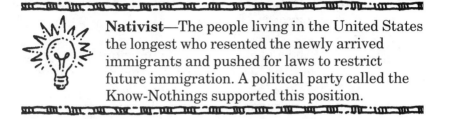

Nativist—The people living in the United States the longest who resented the newly arrived immigrants and pushed for laws to restrict future immigration. A political party called the Know-Nothings supported this position.

This chapter will explore the interrelationship of these features. Sherlock will also take you to the closing of the West and examine what happened to the Indians who lived there.

Look at the definitions, the Time Line of events at the beginning of the chapter, and the Gilded Age Mind Map.

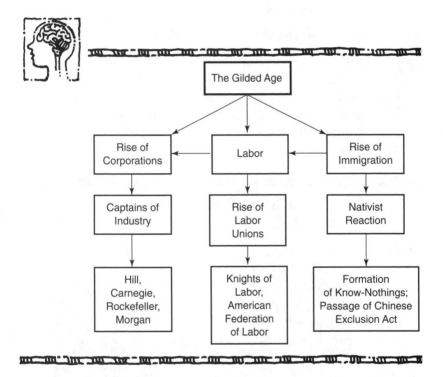

See if you can predict what some of the issues facing the country were during this time period.

CHAPTER FLASHBACK:

At the end of the last chapter, Sherlock spoke about the Reconstruction of the country after the Civil War. A new president, Ulysses S. Grant, became the president responsible for completing the plan passed by Congress.

The definitions, Time Line, and Mind Map should suggest to you the themes of this chapter:

- the rise of industry
- the rise of labor
- the rise of immigration

The issues related to these themes include:

1. what will happen to smaller industries when big corporations take over
2. what workers will do to get better working conditions
3. the impact of immigration on the country
4. the closing of the West and the status of Native Americans

BIOGRAPHY SPOTLIGHT: ULYSSES S. GRANT:

Even though most historians look at Grant as a mediocre president, it is interesting to note that the bulk of Reconstruction took place under his presidency. The ratification of the Fifteenth Amendment, giving the freed slaves the right to vote, and the Amnesty Act, which pretty much normalized relations with the South, were both passed during Grant's administration. He also signed the first Civil Rights Act following the ratification of the

Fourteenth Amendment. And he was angered by the
formation of the Ku Klux Klan, white racists who wore
hoods, burned crosses, and took pride in beating and killing
blacks, Jews, and other minorities. In 1872 Grant pursued
their prosecution, sending a strong message.

HISTORICAL TIDBIT

Since Grant was familiar with the way
things were done in the army, he brought
to the White House a number of his military staff when he
became president.

Unfortunately for Grant, a major scandal called the
Crédit Mobilier Affair hurt his presidency.

Crédit Mobilier Affair—A political scandal
that took place during Grant's presidency in
which congressmen and the vice-president were
bribed to overlook the illegal practices of the
railroad industry.

However, by the time he left office, the country was poised to
start a new chapter in its growth.

THE RISE OF CORPORATIONS

Without a doubt, the major influence during the Gilded Age
came about as a result of the rise of big corporations, driven
by individuals who accumulated large sums of money and
were able to destroy their competition. It started with the
growth of the railroads and ended with industries forming
monopolies and trusts.

Monopoly—The combination of similar industries resulting in the elimination of competition within that industry; also called trusts and combinations.

Early Inventors

Textile Industry—Eli Whitney
Agriculture—Cyrus McCormick
Transportation—Henry Ford
Communication—Alexander G. Bell

Captains of Industry

Beyond the inventors, you should also look at the dominant industrial leaders whom we have previously described as captains of industry, namely Andrew Carnegie, John D. Rockefeller, and Cornelius Vanderbilt. Let's look at each of these individuals. Then Sherlock will send you on a journey to look at their accomplishments.

Andrew Carnegie came to this country as a Scottish immigrant at the age of 12. He first worked in a cotton factory and then on a railroad. Before he was 30 years old, he had already made investments that returned large sums of money. By 1865 he focused his attention on the iron industry and in 1875 he built a steel mill in Pittsburgh, Pennsylvania. Because of the size of his industry, he teamed up with the railroads, received favorable rates, and soon dominated the entire industry. Before he retired, in the 1890s, he merged his holdings with smaller steel companies and became a very wealthy man. At that point he decided to donate some of the money he made to charity. This is called *philanthropy*.

Andrew Carnegie's seven "wisest" fields of philanthropy:

- universities
- free libraries
- hospitals
- parks
- concert halls
- swimming baths
- church buildings

Specifically, the Carnegie name can be found on the following:

Carnegie Hall
Carnegie Institute
Carnegie Mellon University
Carnegie Trust for the Universities of Scotland
Carnegie Institute of Washington
The Carnegie Dunfermline Trust
Carnegie Hero Fund Commission
The Carnegie Foundation for the Advancement of
    Teaching
Carnegie Endowment for International Peace
    Carnegie Corporation of New York
The Carnegie United Kingdom Trust
Carnegie Council for Ethics in International Affairs

Looking at Carnegie's life, it should become obvious that he could be characterized as both a captain of industry and a robber baron. Certainly, the manner in which he dominated the steel industry made him a captain; from the perspective of his workers, he also could be viewed as a robber baron. He was called a philanthropist because of the large sums of money he gave away. Just think about the number of contemporary things named after him—Carnegie Hall in New York City and the Carnegie Foundation, to name just two.

John D. Rockefeller was the founder of Standard Oil Company. He received his business training as a youngster, buying candy at low prices and reselling it to his classmates for a profit. While a teenager, he worked as an accountant for a grocer and impressed his employer with his ability. He had the feeling that oil was going to be one of our most important resources and quickly got involved in the refining of the product. Once he started Standard Oil, he was able to use the profits and expand the business until it became a virtual monopoly. He achieved huge wealth and, like Carnegie, gave away huge sums to charity.

Contributions to Charity—Carnegie vs. Rockefeller			
Year	Newspaper	Carnegie	Rockefeller
1904	The Times of London	$21,000,000	$10,000,000
1910	The New York American	$179,300,000	$134,271,000
1913	The New York Herald	$332,000,000	$175,000,000

Sherlock Question: According to the chart who gave more money to charity?

Cornelius Vanderbilt was king of the railroad industry. He combined 13 railroads in the 1860s, creating a single line connecting New York City and Buffalo. Over the next ten years, he also obtained other lines that went to Chicago, Illinois, and Detroit, Michigan, and the New York Central line. Through these acquisitions Vanderbilt became one of a select group controlling the transportation system of the United States. As a result of the growth of the railroads, small towns grew into large cities and factories sprang up in these new hubs. Vanderbilt accumulated large profits from his business and, to a large extent, became the symbol of what is called the Gilded Age.

HISTORICAL TIDBIT

The Vanderbilts built a burial tomb in Staten Island that cost over a million dollars and was looked after by a full-time watchman.

One of the ways to really see how these great industrialists lived is to visit their homes. Many of them had summer homes in Newport, Rhode Island. The Vanderbilt mansion, The Breakers, is particularly impressive. Visit that home and other mansions at the Newport Mansions web site at:

http://www.NewportMansions.org/

HISTORICAL TIDBIT

Some of the extravagances of the time included a dinner held in honor of a dog that was given a diamond collar. Not to be outdone, men had holes drilled into their teeth so they could have diamonds placed in them.

THE RISE OF THE AMERICAN LABOR MOVEMENT

The history of labor parallels the rise of industry in America, except that, instead of reaping the profits made by big business, the workers generally endured low wages, long hours, and terrible working conditions. It was even worse for women and children. When the nation was hit by poor economic times, the workers suffered more. Added to this was the fact that there was a large immigrant pool of over 18 million between 1880 and 1910. This, along with improved technology, reduced the need for unskilled workers.

One of the interesting theories that contributed to this dilemma was that, given the fact that the United States government pursued a **laissez-faire** capitalism policy, businesses were able to pursue their own interests without fear of government regulation.

Laissez-faire—A hands-off policy adopted by the government regarding the regulation of business.

Add to this the fact that most big business leaders felt that **Social Darwinism** should be the driving force behind their success and you should be able to see why the workers felt they were not receiving their fair share.

Social Darwinism—A theory proposed by John D. Rockefeller that supports the idea that businesses should be able to evolve without government regulation; then the strongest of them would survive.

Unions and the call to strike

So what should the worker do? In one word—organize. Groups of unskilled workers got together and in 1869 formed the first labor union, called the Knights of Labor. The union was open to all workers, including blacks, women, and farmers. At their peak they had over a half-million workers and successfully challenged one of the captains of industry—Jay Gould. However, the union could not maintain its strength and was taken over by a new union led by Samuel Gompers, called the American Federation of Labor (AFL). This was a union only open to skilled workers. It had very simple goals:

increase wages
reduce the number of working hours
improve working conditions

 ## Significant Labor Events 1860–1900

1860—2 million union members

1866—National Labor Union formed by printers, machinists, and stone cutters

1867—Massachusetts instituted first factory inspections for safety hazards.

1869—Knights of Labor formed

1870—Pennsylvania legislature passed first mine safety act in country

1877—Massachusetts enacted worker safety legislation

1882—Railroad workers strike and won demands lost in the strike of 1877

1882—Sept. 5, 1882. First Labor Day celebrated in New York City

1885—Two railroad strike victories help increase Knights of Labor membership to 700,000

1886—the American Federation of Labor formed

1890—Sherman Antitrust Act passed

1892—Strike by steelworkers in Homestead, Pennsylvania, against wage cuts by Carnegie Steel Company was unsuccessful due to use of federal troops and court injunctions

1893—First federal law requiring safety equipment on railroad engines passed

1894—American Railroad Union, led by the socialist Eugene V. Debs, struck a Pullman Car manufacturing plant near Chicago.The federal government took action that led to the defeat of the strike.

The chronology makes it obvious that labor faced difficult times in its early stages. Notice that, for the most part, protests and strikes did not accomplish the goals of lower wages and better working conditions. In some cases, protests led to injuries and even death. The coal-mining laborers known as the Molly Maguires were hanged after protesting in 1877. The labor leader Samuel Gompers had a vision that unskilled workers would be in a weaker position than skilled workers; therefore, he organized only skilled workers into the American Federation of Labor. Eventually, this group merged with another labor organization known as the Congress of Industrial Organization (CIO) to become the largest labor union—the AFL-CIO.

EYEWITNESS ACCOUNT: LIFE AT A CARNEGIE STEEL MILL:

According to Bill Rogel,

Jewelry, you were not allowed to wear any jewelry, if it'd get hot it'd burn your finger. You wasn't allowed to wear a chain around your neck because if the chain got hot and that it would burn you, so any anything like that was forbidden. rings, and chains.

Sherlock Question: How are workers protected today when they are working at their jobs?

The only real tool the labor unions had against the abuses of big business was the strike. Some of the most violent strikes took place during this time period. They included:

The Great Rail Strike of 1877

Workers were upset that the railroad owners were cutting their pay so a strike was called and workers from Baltimore to Pittsburgh left their jobs. Violence between the striking workers and the Pennsylvania state militia broke out. President Rutherford B. Hayes finally sent in federal troops and the strike ended.

The Haymarket Square Riot (1886)

An unidentified individual threw a bomb into a labor meeting that had been called to discuss the strike that was taking place at the McCormick Harvester Company in Chicago. Nine people were killed, and over fifty were injured.

The Homestead Steel Works Strike (1892)

Workers at Carnegie's Pittsburgh plant struck over wages, hours, and working conditions. Carnegie's business partner called out the Pinkerton detectives, and fighting broke out between the workers and the private detectives. Many were killed and injured on both sides.

The Pullman Railroad Strike (1894)

Led by Eugene V. Debs against the Pullman Railroad, this strike spread across the nation as other railroad workers refused to work in a show of support. President Grover Cleveland was forced to send out federal troops to break the strike because the U.S. mails were delayed.

The Homestead strike was one of the most violent in labor history. If you follow the links, you will see that both the labor union and Carnegie would not compromise. The use of the Pinkerton detectives and their strong-arm tactics created a situation in which violence was almost inevitable. Carnegie was viewed by labor as a Judas, while the public at large was also critical of the fact that the workers had to resort to a strike, rather than work things out.

Labor did not begin to see any real government regulation until the reform movement of the early 1900s took hold. However, there were two measures passed by Congress and signed into law that signaled to the captains of industry that the government would step in to break up monopolies. The Interstate Commerce Act (1887) established the Interstate Commerce Commission and put railroads on notice that if they were involved in activities that went beyond the border of one state, they could be regulated. Also, the passage of the Sherman Antitrust Act in 1890 defined a monopoly as a "restraint of trade" and made monopolies illegal. Read more about this in Chapter Eight.

THE RISE OF IMMIGRATION

The story of the immigrant experience should touch each of us. Unless you are of Native American ancestry, somewhere in your family tree, there is a person who immigrated to America.

SHERLOCK ACTIVITY: CREATE YOUR OWN FAMILY TREE:

Using the diagram below, make your own family tree.

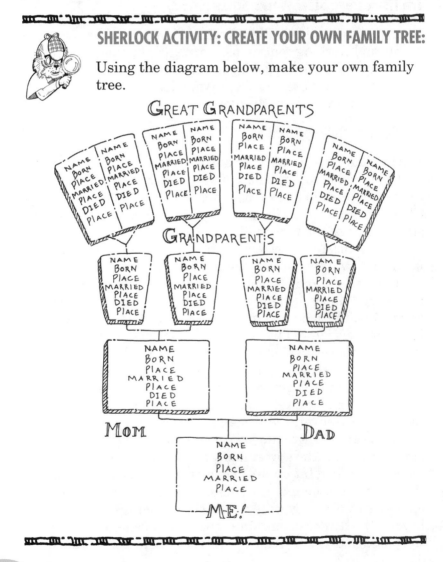

The search for one's family roots is as old as the family itself. By using the form provided by "Onlinegenealogy" and following the directions it provides, you can begin the process of building your family tree. In addition, talk to your parents and grandparents and see how far back they can go tracing where their relatives came from. Compare your findings with your friends.

Immigrants came to this country for a variety of reasons—social, economic, and political. Remember that the first colonists who came from England left there for religious reasons. The Irish came in the 1840s because of a potato famine, and many people came from Russia to escape the tyranny of the Czar.

In many cases, the people living outside the United States had a vision that the streets here were paved with gold, and this perception was advanced many times when former countrymen returned with the stories that they told.

SHERLOCK EYEWITNESS ACCOUNT:

For every immigrant who came to this country, there was a story of hope and prayer. The entry point for immigrants arriving on the East Coast was Ellis Island in New York. The island was the central repository for arriving immigrants and the first site most immigrants saw as they entered New York harbor was the Statue of Liberty.

How would you feel about arriving in America at Ellis Island?

First-person immigrant accounts provide an interesting source explaining why immigrants chose to leave their homeland. In the case of Chinese immigrant Lee Chew, it was hearing from a villager who had left to go to America as a young boy; when he returned, he was much wealthier than the rest of the villagers. It supported the idea that the streets of America were paved with gold. But don't forget that there were really serious reasons for immigrants choosing to leave their homeland. From the 1840s to 1880s Germans left because there was an economic depression and political tyranny in their country. In the 1870s and 1900s Scandinavian immigrants left because of economic hardship in Denmark, Sweden, Norway, and Finland. From the 1880s to the 1920s Italian immigrants left Italy because of economic hardship. During the same period, Jews from Eastern Europe came to America to escape political oppression and religious persecution. There was also the Asian migration to the West Coast during the height of immigration, between 1888 and 1920.

The official home page of Ellis Island is:

http://www.ellisisland.org/

There you will be able to visit the museum that is currently located on the island and you will also be able to see if your relatives are inscribed on the Immigrant's Wall of Honor.

Immigrants faced common problems after they arrived in America. Take a look at the immigration Mind Map to get a complete understanding of the obstacles facing immigrants.

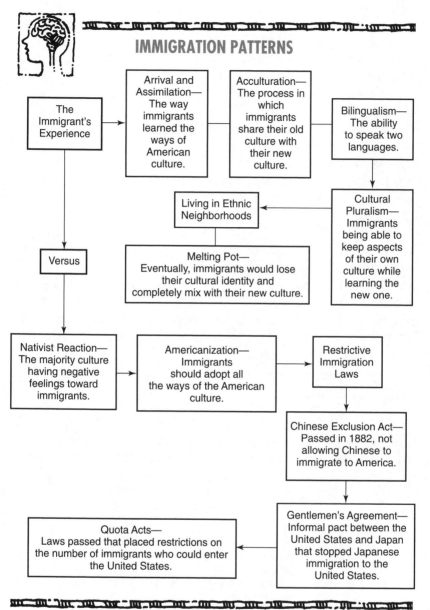

IMMIGRATION PATTERNS

The Immigrant's Experience

Arrival and Assimilation— The way immigrants learned the ways of American culture.

Acculturation— The process in which immigrants share their old culture with their new culture.

Bilingualism— The ability to speak two languages.

Cultural Pluralism— Immigrants being able to keep aspects of their own culture while learning the new one.

Living in Ethnic Neighborhoods

Melting Pot— Eventually, immigrants would lose their cultural identity and completely mix with their new culture.

Versus

Nativist Reaction— The majority culture having negative feelings toward immigrants.

Americanization— Immigrants should adopt all the ways of the American culture.

Restrictive Immigration Laws

Chinese Exclusion Act— Passed in 1882, not allowing Chinese to immigrate to America.

Gentlemen's Agreement— Informal pact between the United States and Japan that stopped Japanese immigration to the United States.

Quota Acts— Laws passed that placed restrictions on the number of immigrants who could enter the United States.

Guess which side wins out—the successful assimilation and eventual melting pot of the immigrant, or nativists succeeding in putting a halt to immigration.

The basic question regarding the issue of immigration— and it still is posed today—is whether the words from Emma

Lazarus's poem found at the beginning of this chapter, "*Give us your tired, your poor, your huddled masses . . .* " is accepted by the people and government of the United States. If you look at the immigration Mind Map, and understand the definitions of terms related to the topic, you should see that the answer to the question is a difficult one. On the one hand, since the vast majority of us are immigrants, we don't want to deprive new immigrants from having the same opportunities as our relatives had. On the other hand, there are limited resources this country can provide, and many people feel that the number of illegal aliens has also been on the rise.

Once the immigrant settled in the new country, the most important accomplishment was getting a job. Because of the need for cheap labor, Chinese immigrants were used to build the transcontinental railroad. Other immigrant groups were hired to work in factories. Most immigrants also settled in the cities, and, as a result, cities began to take on a life of their own. To get a complete picture of immigration patterns visit the U.S. Census site at:

http://www.census.gov

There you will be able to trace immigration patterns and see when immigrants came to the United States and where they settled.

THE FATE OF THE INDIANS AND THE CLOSING OF THE WEST

As the Indians were pushed further and further west, increasingly there were conflicts between many of the tribes and the pioneers moving to the lands opened up by the government. Some of the more notable encounters took place with the Sioux of the Northern Plains and the Apache of the Southwest. Indian leaders, such as Red Cloud and Crazy

Horse, waged an all-out war with the cavalry and white settlers. In retaliation, and for sport, the whites hunted one of the Indian's most important resources, the buffalo. The government passed laws restricting the tribes to reserva-tions.

The encounter that illustrates the bitter confrontation between the two forces took place in 1876 when the Sioux war reached its peak. After the Dakota gold rush ushered in an influx of miners, the cavalry was given orders to keep the miners off Sioux hunting grounds; however, nothing was done to protect the Indian land itself. The Sioux attacked and the army, led by General George Custer, moved in at Little Big Horn. His unit was wiped out. Then in the celebration at Wounded Knee, the Sioux were attacked and hundreds died including men and women.

SHERLOCK EYEWITNESS ACCOUNT: THE BATTLE OF LITTLE BIG HORN:

by the Lakota Chief Red Horse

The day was hot. In a short time the soldiers charged the camp. [This was Maj. Reno's battalion of the Seventh Cavalry.] The soldiers came on the trail made by the Sioux camp in moving, and crossed the Little Bighorn river above where the Sioux crossed, and attacked the lodges of the Uncpapas, farthest up the river. The women and children ran down the Little Bighorn river a short distance into a ravine. The soldiers set fire to the lodges. All the Sioux now charged the soldiers and drove them in confusion across the Little Bighorn river, which was very rapid, and several soldiers were drowned in it. On a hill the soldiers stopped and the Sioux surrounded them. A Sioux man came and said that a different party of Soldiers had all the women and children prisoners. Like a whirlwind the word went around, and the Sioux all heard it and left the soldiers on the hill and went quickly to save the women and children.

Sherlock Question: Why was the Battle of Little Big Horn called *Custer's Last Stand?*

Custer's Last Stand was one of the saddest events in the relations between the United States and the Native American tribes. Unfortunately, the battle did not end the hostilities between the two sides, and, very shortly thereafter, the massacre at Wounded Knee occurred.

 HISTORICAL TIDBIT

Custer led his troops at Little Big Horn even though his superiors had ordered him not to go there.

Two other events reflect the sad history of the Native Americans. After Little Big Horn, the last of the great Apache chiefs, Geronimo, waged wars in the Southwest. He was captured in 1885. The Dawes Act, passed vin 1887, attempted to make the government more responsible about the treatment of Indians. As well intentioned as the law was, Native American land was still seized and tribal culture was not honored.

As the Native Americans were being pushed into reservations, the West itself was shrinking. The California gold rush in the 1840s, the Oregon settlement in the 1870s, and the move to settle in the Southwest resulted in the closing of the frontier.

A new American character emerged shaped by the West. By the time California was settled, the final frontier had been reached.

Now let's look at the presidents who led this country during the Gilded Age. Each of the presidents contributed greatly to this time period. Some of the facts you could find out by exploring the site include:

Rutherford Birchard Hayes (1877–1881)—He was named the "dark horse" president because even though his opponent won a majority of the popular votes, he won a majority of the electoral votes.

James Abram Garfield (1881)—He was assassinated by an unhappy government worker who felt that he deserved a better position.

Chester Alan Arthur (1881–1885)—Because he took over the presidency after Garfield's assassination, Arthur never delivered a formal inaugural address.

Grover Cleveland (1885–1889 and 1893–1897)—He was the only president to be elected for two *nonconsecutive* terms.

SHERLOCKS MATCHING MADNESS:

Match the name of the labor strike with the description of the strike.

The Great Rail Strike of 1877	Workers at Carnegie's Pittsburgh plant struck over wages, hours, and working conditions.
The Haymarket Square Riot of 1886	Led by Eugene V. Debs, this strike spread across the nation as other railroad workers refused to work.
The Homewood Steel Worker's Strike of 1892	President Rutherford B. Hayes sent in federal troops to end this strike.
The Pullman Railroad Strike of 1894	Nine people were killed after a bomb was set off at a labor meeting in Chicago.

CHAPTER EIGHT

The Emergence of Modern America (1898–1929)

BIG STICK

CARIBBEAN SEA

Intellectually I know that America is no better than any other country; emotionally I know she is better than every other country.

—author Sinclair Lewis

Time Line (1898–1929)

1898 Battleship *Maine* explodes in Havana Harbor

1898 Spanish-American War begins

1898 Annexation of Hawaii

1898 Treaty ends Spanish-American War

1899 United States acquires Puerto Rico and Guam

1899 Cuba becomes U.S. territory

1900 William McKinley reelected president

1901 McKinley assassinated; Theodore Roosevelt becomes president

1902 Philippines become U.S. territory

1902 United States gives Cuba independence

1903 Panama Canal treaty passed

1904 Theodore Roosevelt elected president

1905 *The Jungle* published

1906 Pure Food and Drug Act passed

1908 William Howard Taft elected president

1909 National Association for the Advancement of Colored People (NAACP) formed

1912 Woodrow Wilson elected president

1913 Sixteenth Amendment ratified

1913 Seventeenth Amendment ratified

1913 Ford sets up first automobile assembly line

1913 Panama Canal completed

1914 World War I begins

1914 United States declares neutrality

1915 *Lusitania* sunk by German submarine

1916 Woodrow Wilson reelected president

1917 The United States enters World War I

1917 Eighteenth Amendment ratified

1918 Wilson announces Fourteen Points

1918 World War I ends

1919 Treaty of Versailles signed

1919 Senate rejects Treaty of Versailles

1919 Nineteenth Amendment ratified

1920 Sacco-Vanzetti trial

1920 Warren Harding elected president

1921 Restrictive immigration law passed

1921 Ku Klux Klan on the rise

1922 Teapot Dome scandal

1923 Harding dies in office; Coolidge becomes new president

1924 Coolidge reelected president

1925 Scopes Monkey Trial

1927 Lindbergh flies solo across the Atlantic

1928 Herbert Hoover elected president

1929 Stock Market crashes

THE PROGRESSIVE MOVEMENT

The causes

The Progressive Movement, unparalleled in American history, brought about significant social, economic, and political changes from 1900 to the outbreak of World War I.

CHAPTER FLASHBACK:

In the last chapter Sherlock looked at the causes and consequences of an American nation that increased its industrial output. We spoke of captains of industry and robber barons, and we looked at why this nation struggled with the fact that even though we were a nation on the move, there still were serious problems to deal with.

Let's review some of these problems:

- the rise of monopolies and the abuses brought about by the industrialization of the United States after the Civil War
- the growth of cities stemming from the Industrial Revolution
- monopolies created by Rockefeller, Swift, Carnegie, and other industrial barons
- poor living conditions in cities
- conflict between business and labor unions
- abuse of child labor and women

The key word that describes the new era in American history, the **Progressive Era,** is reform.

The Progressive Era—The time in America from 1898 to 1918 when political, social, and economic reform resulted in progress in those institutions of American life.

But don't forget that this country had a history of reform movements that occurred in the United States during the nineteenth century such as:

the **abolitionist** movement
the **women's suffrage** movement
the **temperance** movement, advocating the prohibition of alcohol
Civil Service Reform motivated by the assassination of President Garfield
The **Granger movement** which led to the rise of the **Populist party** in the 1880s

Abolitionist Movement—Antislave organizers led by Theodore Weld and William Lloyd Garrison, who favored the immediate freedom of all slaves from 1830 until the adoption of the Fourteenth Amendment.

Women's suffrage movement—led by Elizabeth Cady Stanton, Lucretia Mott, and Susan B. Anthony, who demonstrated for the right to vote for women. In 1848 at Seneca Falls, New York, a Declaration of Rights and Sentiments was signed urging full equality, including the right to vote for women.

Temperance Movement—organizers favored making alcohol illegal. This was known as prohibition. The Eighteenth Amendment passed in 1919. It banned the distribution of alcohol in the United States. The amendment was repealed by the Twenty-First Amendment in 1936.

Civil Service Reform—The assassination of President Garfield by an angry individual who was denied a government job, led to the passage of the Pendleton Act in 1883. This act reformed many of the abuses of what was called, "the spoils system," giving politicians the right to appoint people to government jobs.

Granger Movement—Organized by farmers who objected to high railroad rates. They pressured state lawmakers to pass laws regulating these rates. These laws were called Granger laws.

Populist Party—Founded in 1890 as an outgrowth of the Granger Movement, this third political party believed in reform of the political, economic, and social institutions of this country.

Specifically, the party developed a platform, or statement of beliefs, that favored:

- an income tax that would tax the people who made more money at a higher rate than those who earned lower income, called a *graduated income tax*
- government ownership of railroads
- direct election of senators
- the passage of laws that would create an eight-hour workday
- state laws that would reform the political process by allowing the **initiative, referendum, and recall**

Initiative, referendum, and recall
Initiative–Voters decide what kind of laws they want to vote on.
Referendum—The actual ballot proposal that the voters decide.
Recall—The right of the voters to remove an elected official from office.

Look at the Progressive Era Mind Map and the Time Line at the beginning of the chapter. Explain why this is such an important period in American history.

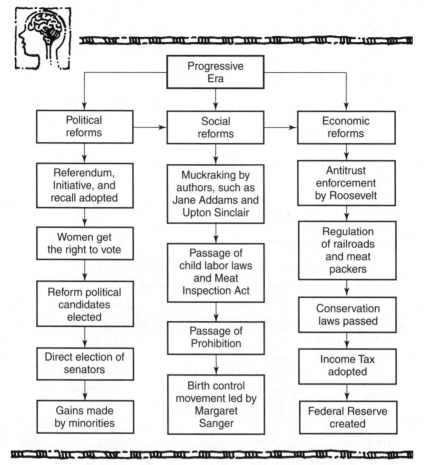

```
                    ┌─────────────┐
                    │ Progressive │
                    │    Era      │
                    └─────────────┘
```

Political reforms	Social reforms	Economic reforms
Referendum, Initiative, and recall adopted	Muckraking by authors, such as Jane Addams and Upton Sinclair	Antitrust enforcement by Roosevelt
Women get the right to vote	Passage of child labor laws and Meat Inspection Act	Regulation of railroads and meat packers
Reform political candidates elected	Passage of Prohibition	Conservation laws passed
Direct election of senators	Birth control movement led by Margaret Sanger	Income Tax adopted
Gains made by minorities		Federal Reserve created

The Progressive Era Mind Map and the Time Line should give you an idea of the scope and importance of this time period. The words that should come to your mind when you hear of this era are *progress* and *reform*. The map concentrates on three areas of reform—political, social, and economic. And the chronology emphasizes specific events that correspond to the Mind Map outline. As you read more details of this chapter, you should be able to figure out why this period is so significant.

The Progressive Era presidents

The best way to measure the results of the Progressive Era is to look at who was president; then you must look at the reform measures that were passed. One reason why these presidents favored reform of social, political, and economic institutions was because of what is called the motivators of change—the **muckrakers**.

Muckrakers—Writers during the Progressive Era who, through their works, stressed the social, economic, and political abuses facing the country.

These writers included:

1. **Lincoln Steffens.** He wrote *The Shame of the Cities,* which told how corrupt city politicians were.
2. **Ida Tarbell.** She investigated John D. Rockefeller's Standard Oil Company in her book *History of Standard Oil Company.*
3. **Upton Sinclair.** He wrote a novel, *The Jungle,* which outlined the abuses in the meat packing industry and resulted in passage of the Meat Inspection Act and the Pure Food and Drug Act in 1906.
4. Magazines such as *McClures,* which published numerous articles. One such article appeared in 1894 and was titled "In the Depths of a Coal Mine" by Stephen Crane.

 SHERLOCK EYEWITNESS ACCOUNT:

The room shrieks and blares and bellows. Clouds of dust blur the air . . . Down in the midst of it sit these tiny urchins, where they earn fifty-five cents a day each. They breathe this atmosphere until their lungs grow heavy and sick with it.
—"In the Depths of a Coal Mine" by Stephen Crane

Sherlock's Question: How does this account fit the definition of muckraking?

The eyewitness description uses graphic words to point out the terrible working conditions these coal miners faced. As a result of this article, there was an outcry for better working conditions in the coal mines. Eventually, legislation was passed to improve conditions.

Let's now take a look at the Progressive presidents and what they accomplished during their administrations. We will deal with President McKinley separately when we look at the Spanish-American War later in this chapter.

Theodore Roosevelt (1901–1909)

- His administration advocated a "Square Deal" to the American people. He became known as a champion of reform and a "trustbuster." He went after Standard Oil, Swift and Company, and Northern Securities.
- He helped settle the coal strike.
- He regulated the railroads and meatpackers through the Meat Inspection Act, Pure Food and Drug Act, Elkins Act, and Hepburn Act.
- He became known as a conservationist, signing into law the Newlands Reclamation Act in 1902 and the Inland Waterways Act.

William Howard Taft (1909–1913)

- He was also known as a trustbuster, breaking up over 90 businesses.
- Reformers felt betrayed when he raised tariffs and when he fired a leading conservationist, Gifford Pinchot.

Woodrow Wilson (1913–1921)

- Though known primarily as the president who led us through World War I, his administration also played a key role in the Progressive Era. His program for change, The New Freedom, advocated lower tariffs, regulation of big business, and a reform of the banking industry.
- During his administration the Clayton Antitrust Act was passed (it strengthened the Sherman Antitrust Act by specifically outlawing certain types

of corporations). He established the Federal Trade Commission and instituted the Federal Reserve System, a national bank that helps to regulate the nation's money supply.

 **HISTORICAL PRESIDENTIAL TIDBITS:**

Theodore Roosevelt—Had the nickname "TR" and led the Rough Riders during the Spanish-American War.
William Howard Taft—The only president to serve as chief justice of the Supreme Court after he left office.
Woodrow Wilson—Won the election of 1912 because Theodore Roosevelt ran as a third-party candidate from the Bull Moose party, thereby splitting the Republican vote.

As a result of the efforts of muckrakers and these three presidents, the most significant reforms were passed. Besides the laws already mentioned, constitutional amendments were passed: The Sixteenth Amendment allowed a graduated income tax, the Seventeenth Amendment instituted the direct election of senators, the Eighteenth Amendment brought Prohibition, and the Nineteenth Amendment gave women the right to vote. The significance of this reform movement can still be felt in our lives today.

AN EMERGING GLOBAL NATION

The Spanish-American War

The Spanish-American War was a turning point in American foreign policy. It was an event that symbolized America's new thirst for land and resources. It also gave a signal to the rest of the world that our traditional foreign policy of neutrality and isolationism had evolved into a more aggressive role.

Let's look at the background events leading to the war:

- Manifest destiny was completed. Through diplomacy such as the Louisiana Purchase, annexation, and war such as the Mexican War, we expanded our territory to the West Coast by the late 1800s. This movement was aided by the building of the transcontinental railroad and the movement of Indians to reservations.
- Trade became important as the nation became industrialized. In 1887 we were granted naval rights to Hawaii. By 1898 we annexed Hawaii. We also had an interest in the Samoan Islands. We supported a more open trading policy with China and also traded with Japan, starting in 1853 when Commodore Perry negotiated a trade agreement.
- Motivated by our own industrialization, it became an unstated goal of the United States to pursue a policy that some would characterize as imperialism—seeking foreign land for resources.

Factors That Led the United States to War

- In 1895 Cuban nationals staged a revolt against Spanish rule. Americans were highly sympathetic to the Cuban people.
- **Yellow Journalism,** led by the efforts of William Randolph Hearst, whose *New York Journal* used screaming headlines to stir up the emotions of the American people.

 Yellow Journalism—Newspaper reporting that uses screaming headlines to make a point. Practiced by William Randolph Hearst, an example of this kind of journalism was the headline "Remember the Maine."

- **The De Lome letter.** The Spanish minister to the United States, William De Lome, wrote a secret letter calling President McKinley weak and ineffective. Hearst got a copy of the letter and printed it in his newspaper. This outraged the American people.

- **The sinking of the U.S.S. *Maine*.** This key event, made worse by the headline "Remember the Maine," suggested that the battleship *Maine* was blown up in the harbor at Havana by Spain, killing 250 Americans. The newspaper stories made it seem that it was Spain's fault, even though it was never proven that Spain, in fact, was responsible. Ironically, after an inquiry, it is believed that the ship either struck a mine or had an internal accident.

SHERLOCK EYEWITNESS ACCOUNT: SINKING OF THE *MAINE*:

"I laid down my pen and listened to the notes of the bugle, which were singularly beautiful in the oppressive stillness of the night. . . .
I was enclosing my letter in its envelope when the explosion came. It was a bursting, rending, and crashing roar of immense volume, largely metallic in character. It was followed by heavy, ominous metallic sounds. There was a trembling and lurching motion of the vessel, a list to port. The electric lights went out. Then there was intense blackness and smoke.
The situation could not be mistaken. The Maine *was blown up and sinking. For a moment the instinct of self-preservation took charge of me, but this was immediately dominated by the habit of command.*
—Captain Charles Sigsbee

Sherlock's Question: How did the sinking of the *Maine* result in "yellow journalism"?

The Declaration of War

Though Spain promised eventual Cuban independence, public opinion favored war. There was a significant amount of economic investment in Cuba. The military liked the idea that Cuba could provide a naval base. In April, 1898, President William McKinley asked Congress for a declaration of war.

HISTORICAL TIDBIT

William Randolph Hearst, whose newspapers were known for "yellow journalism," responded to a friend who indicated that all was quiet in Cuba: "If you furnish the pictures, I'll furnish the war."

HISTORICAL TIDBIT

McKinley was assassinated within a year after the start of his second term.

The "Splendid Little War"

The war has been called the "Splendid Little War" and what follows is a summary of the highlights:

- It lasted four months.
- It was fought in the Western Hemisphere in Cuba and Puerto Rico, and also in the Philippines in the Pacific.
- It brought to fame Theodore Roosevelt and the Rough Riders in a famous battle charge up San Juan Hill. Roosevelt's leadership brought down Spain in Puerto Rico and Cuba.

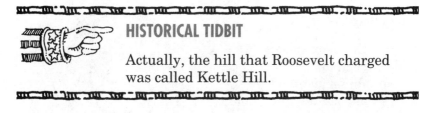

HISTORICAL TIDBIT

Actually, the hill that Roosevelt charged was called Kettle Hill.

- In the Philippines, Commodore George Dewey led the naval fleet to Manila where he won an easy victory.

Unlike other wars, the Spanish-American War was fought by the United States in an effort to gain new territory. Actually, we defeated Spain in a short period of time. Our forces were led by Theodore Roosevelt and Commodore Dewey. The links on these sites take you through the chronology of the war and give you interesting pictures of the battles. Some historians call this type of aggression *imperialism*. Besides fighting the war, the United States also pursued this policy as we gained rights to build a canal in Panama and ruled the Philippines.

The Treaty of Paris (1899)

- Spain granted independence to Cuba and gave Puerto Rico and Guam to the United States. Spain sold the Philippines to the United States for $20 million.
- Though a clear and convincing victory, the country became split between imperialists led by Theodore Roosevelt and anti-imperialists led by William Jennings Bryan. Their arguments centered over the fact that we put down a Filipino Revolution and set up a government in the Philippines responsible to the United States. Though Cuba was granted its independence, the Platt Amendment created certain conditions including the establishment of a U.S. naval base in Cuba and continuing United States influence in Cuba even after it became independent.
- Puerto Rico became a commonwealth and remains so to this day, although there is a movement to let the people decide whether the island should become a state.

The Significance of the War

- The United States established itself as a global power.
- We became a "big brother" to Latin America. This became more formalized during Theodore Roosevelt's administration as he established a doctrine that he described as the Big Stick policy.

TEDDY ROOSEVELT

WORLD WAR I

President Wilson was elected during the height of the Progressive Era in 1912, but by 1914 he and the country faced a new crisis—the first modern world war that broke out in Europe in 1914. Though Wilson stated that the United States would officially be neutral, most of the efforts of industry and banks favored the allies of Great Britain and France against Germany.

Germany responded in 1915 by announcing a policy of unrestricted submarine warfare against all merchant ships. The United States protested and threatened to respond if Germany attacked our ships. In 1915 Germany sank the British liner *Lusitania,* which had 1,200 people on board including 128 Americans. The United States expressed outrage and Germany backed off, ordering their submarines to give warnings in the future before attacking. By  1916, however, these orders were ignored and unrestricted submarine warfare continued. Wilson issued Germany an ultimatum, threatening United States involvement in the war, and for the moment Germany again backed down. As a result, Wilson was re-elected, using a political slogan: "He kept us out of war."

In 1917 Germany again announced a policy of unrestricted submarine warfare and carried it out by sinking five U.S. ships. That act, plus the fact that the allies were having a difficult time defeating Germany, made Wilson call for a declaration of war.

Look at two of Wilson's main arguments for declaring war against Germany. He stated,

"I want to make the world safe for democracy."
"This will be the war to end all wars."

How do you think the country and Congress reacted to his request for a declaration of war?

Language like that of Wilson resonated with the American people. As we became more and more involved in the war, our presence made a big difference in the outcome. Near the end of the war, we had almost two million soldiers overseas.

World War I Casualties			
Country	Number of Troops	Dead	Wounded
Russia	12,000,000	1,700,000	4,950,000
Germany	11,000,000	1,773,700	4,216,058
Great Britain	8,904,467	908,371	2,090,212
France	8,410,000	1,375,800	4,266,000
Austria-Hungary	7,800,000	1,200,000	3,620,000

World War I Casualties (*continued*)			
Country	Number of Troops	Dead	Wounded
Italy	5,615,000	650,000	947,000
United States	4,355,000	126,000	234,300
Turkey	2,850,000	325,000	400,000
Bulgaria	1,200,000	87,500	152,390
Japan	800,000	300	907
Romania	750,000	335,706	120,000
Serbia	707,343	45,000	133,148
Belgium	267,000	13,716	44,686
Greece	230,000	5,000	21,000
Portugal	100,000	7,222	13,751
Montenegro	50,000	3,000	10,000

Sherlock's Question: What conclusions can you reach by looking at this chart?

Visit World War I web site, World War I—Trenches, on the web at:
This site contains a narrative of the war with eyewitness

http://www.worldwar1.com/

accounts, weapons of the war, including the use of chemical warfare, music of the war, posters, sound recordings, and statistics dealing with the casualties.

This war, although it was fought in Europe, placed a great burden on the United States. For the first time, the country faced trench warfare and chemical weapons, such as mustard gas, and it was the first war in which airplanes were used. The country reacted positively, however, and had confidence in President Wilson.

Wilson was a visionary in regard to what he believed should be the terms for peace. He stated them in what became known as the Fourteen Points. He called for:

- the abolition of secret international agreements
- a guarantee of freedom of the seas
- removal of tariff restrictions between nations
- a lowering of the arms buildup

- the approval of a League of Nations that would guarantee future peace

SHERLOCK DOCUMENT QUEST

The Treaty of Versailles—Creation of the League of Nations:

The Covenant of the League of Nations

THE HIGH CONTRACTING PARTIES, *In order to promote international co-operation and to achieve international peace and security by the acceptance of obligations not to resort to war by the prescription of open, just and honourable relations between nations by the firm establishment of the understandings of international law as the actual rule of conduct among Governments, and by the maintenance of justice and a scrupulous respect for all treaty obligations in the dealings of organised peoples with one another Agree to this Covenant of the League of Nations.*

Sherlock's Question: What was the purpose of the League of Nations?

The Treaty of Versailles

When the war ended in 1918, a treaty was signed in Versailles, France. It included only parts of Wilson's Fourteen Points and treated Germany as the villain, imposing harsh penalties on the defeated nation. Wilson came away with the League of Nations he had wanted but had the difficult job of selling it to the United States Senate. Opposition was led by Republican Senator Henry Cabot Lodge of Massachusetts.

Do you think the United States Senate should have adopted the Treaty of Versailles? What does its rejection show you about the principle of separation of powers? **Hint:** The Senate rejection guaranteed that the United States would not participate in the League of Nations.

Wilson embarked on a national tour arguing for the adoption of the treaty. In the end, the Senate rejected it. Wilson, physically exhausted, suffered a stroke and finished out his second term disabled; however, his legacy, according to presidential scholars, was a positive one. He has been ranked as one of the great presidents.

 HISTORICAL TIDBIT

Even though he was recovering from a stroke, Wilson expressed the desire to be nominated for a third term. Though the convention was deadlocked, Wilson's name was never submitted for consideration.

THE ROARING TWENTIES

The Roaring Twenties, also known as the "Jazz Age," "Age of Prohibition," and "The Return to Normalcy," had a profound impact on American life and particularly on race relations. Socially, economically, and politically, the decade of the twenties reflected a new age of morality that can be evaluated in both a positive and negative manner.

The age was also characterized by the following:

- an age of prosperity—Rising middle class, urban development
- more leisure time—Young women, called "flappers," adopted a flashy manner of dress. The jazz age began, an energetic new dance called the "Charleston" became all the rage, and the popularity of motion pictures grew.
- automobiles and assembly lines—Model T assembly line developed by Henry Ford
- gangster Al Capone in a war against a police unit known as "The Untouchables"

- passage of the Eighteenth Amendment—Prohibition— later repealed by the Twenty-first Amendment
- passage of restrictive immigration legislation
- conflict between a "loose society" and a "moralistic society"

The return to normalcy and presidential politics

Immediately following the end of World War I, the election of 1920 took place. Republican Warren Harding easily beat his Democratic opponent James Cox on a platform of returning the country to "normalcy." This meant that the age of progressivism had ended and there was a return to the laissez-faire policy of the late 1880s and 1890s.

Teapot Dome Scandal

A negative aspect of the twenties, the Teapot Dome referred to federally owned land in Wyoming that had huge oil reserves. Harding's secretary of state, Albert Fall, leased the lands to several oil companies and, in return, received illegal payments. Harding's administration was beset by scandal, including stories that he had a mistress. The president died in office in 1923 and was succeeded by Calvin Coolidge, known as "Silent Cal."

The administration of Calvin Coolidge was characterized by his famous quote that "the business of America is business," referring to the traditional Republican economic policies of high tariffs and the protection of American business.

The last president of the Roaring Twenties, Herbert Hoover, was elected in 1928. Hoover beat the first Roman Catholic to run for president, Alfred E. Smith. The election reflected a prejudice against Roman Catholics and illustrated some of the racial and ethnic prejudice that existed at the time. One event that stood out during Hoover's administration was the stock market crash in 1929.

HISTORICAL PRESIDENTIAL TIDBITS:

Warren G. Harding—The "G" in Warren Harding's name stands for the biblical name Gamaliel.
Calvin Coolidge—His nickname was "Silent Cal."
Herbert Hoover—Herbert Hoover's victory over Al Smith was reversed four years later by almost the identical electoral vote when he lost to Franklin Roosevelt during the height of the depression.

All three Republican presidents believed that government policy should favor big business and did very little to further race relations. In fact, because of the social climate, nativist reaction against immigrants and a fear that communism would spread to the United States—called a *red scare*—characterized the decade.

Social changes

Positive social developments included the following:

- the rise of the middle class, the invention of the telephone, silent movies, the first automobiles, Henry Ford's assembly line, the rise of the city, and the ability of the middle class to partake in leisure activities, creating a new American culture.

HISTORICAL TIDBIT

The expansion of freedom for women was brought on by the passage of the Nineteenth Amendment in 1920, which gave women the right to vote.

Influential Women Suffragists

Susan B. Anthony (1820–1906)
Alice Stone Blackwell (1857–1950)
Antoinette Brown Blackwell (1825–1921)
Harriet Stanton Blatch (1856–1940)

Amelia Bloomer (1818–1894)
Carrie Chapman Catt (1859–1947)
Charlotte Perkins Gilman (1860–1935)
Julia Ward Howe (1819–1910)
Lucretia Coffin Mott (1793–1880)
Anna Howard Shaw (1847–1919)
Elizabeth Cady Stanton (1815–1902)
Lucy Stone (1818–1893)
Sojourner Truth (1797–1883)

- Women also took on the "flapper look," dancing the Charleston, and for the first time smoking in public.
- The Harlem Renaissance was a movement that was characterized by a rise of cultural activities in Harlem and by jazz artists performing at the Apollo Theater.

Moral Dilemmas

- The passage of the Eighteenth Amendment, which prohibited alcohol, was brought on by the Temperance Movement and had a negative effect on the country. Why do you think it was inevitable that Prohibition would fail? Even though Prohibition was the law of the land during the 1920s, it was constantly broken by individuals who made alcohol in their bathtubs, it was violated by bootleggers and such gangsters as Al Capone, and alcohol was easily available in illegal bars called "speakeasies," which became a way of life. You can conclude that it was very difficult to enforce a law that dealt with a moral issue.
- Anger by religious groups spilled over into other areas of American life, such as education. A good example of this was the Scopes Trial, also known as the Scopes Monkey Trial. It took place in Tennessee and involved a schoolteacher whose name was John Scopes. Scopes believed that as a science teacher he should be able to teach Darwin's theory of evolution, but Tennessee had a law that prohibited the teaching of evolution and, instead, directed teachers to teach creationism. Scopes violated the law and the trial became one of the first "trials of the century." Two famous attorneys,

Clarence Darrow, representing Scopes, and former presidential candidate, William Jennings Bryan, arguing the case for Tennessee, battled each other. Though Darrow outmaneuvered Bryan, Scopes lost the case. Both Prohibition and the Scopes trial reflect conflicting moral values.

EDITORIAL CARTOON: THE SCOPES MONKEY TRIAL:

DEFENCE OF EVOLUTION

DARROW

Sherlock's Question: Why was the trial called the Scopes "Monkey Trial"?

Other negative developments of the time included:

• Nativist reaction against immigrants:

1. Passage of anti-immigration laws, such as the Quota Laws of 1921, 1924, and 1929. These laws set strict quotas on immigration into the country.
2. The rise of the Ku Klux Klan. The Klan was comprised of southern whites who terrorized freed slaves after the Civil War. Its new incarnation expanded its hatred against Jews, Catholics, and immigrants.

3. The Red Scare was an outgrowth of the Palmer Commission and was aimed at those individuals who were perceived as favoring communism.

4. The Sacco-Vanzetti trial where two Italian immigrants were accused of murder and armed robbery and convicted based on questionable evidence, illustrated what prejudice and hatred can do. It was later revealed that their conviction came about because they were anarchists and immigrants.

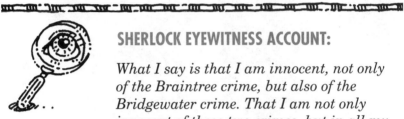

SHERLOCK EYEWITNESS ACCOUNT:

What I say is that I am innocent, not only of the Braintree crime, but also of the Bridgewater crime. That I am not only innocent of these two crimes, but in all my life I have never stolen and I have never killed and I have never spilled blood. That is what I want to say. And it is not all. Not only am I innocent of these two crimes, not only in all my life I have never stolen, never killed, never spilled blood, but I have struggled all my life, since I began to reason, to eliminate crime from the earth.
—Statement from Bartolomeo Vanzetti

Sherlock's Question: What kind of statement did Vanzetti make at the time of his sentencing?

- Race riots in the North as a result of black migration to large cities and continued segregation. Marcus Garvey, a black activist, urged African-Americans to take pride in their heritage. A Return to Africa movement grew out of Garvey's organization. Along with Garvey, black leaders, such as Booker T. Washington and W.E.B. Du Bois also argued that blacks should strive for greater involvement in American society.

The Roaring Twenties, in the end, had a profound impact on American society. Though there were many negatives, especially regarding racial minorities and immigrants, it was an age that finally saw the emergence of a middle class that was able to take advantage of the economic prosperity of the time.

 SHERLOCK'S MATCHING MADNESS:

Match the Progressive movement person with his or her accomplishment.

Lincoln Steffens	Wrote *History of Standard Oil*
Ida Tarbell	Wrote *The Jungle*
Upton Sinclair	Wrote article in *McClures* magazine, "In the Depths of a Coal Mine"
Stephen Crane	Wrote "Shame of the Cities"
Theodore Roosevelt	Program for change called the New Freedom
William Howard Taft	Administration called the Square Deal
Woodrow Wilson	Fired a leading conservationist

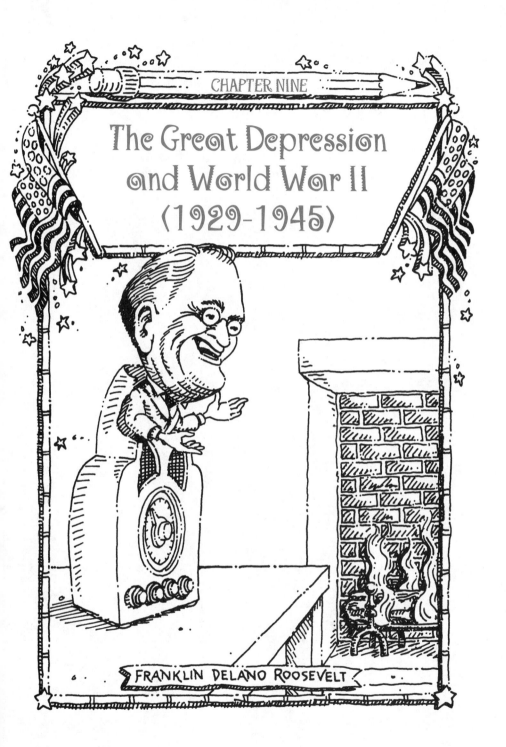

CHAPTER NINE

The Great Depression and World War II (1929-1945)

FRANKLIN DELANO ROOSEVELT

The only thing we have to fear is fear itself.
—Franklin Delano Roosevelt, Inaugural Address, 1933

Time Line (1929–1945)

1930 Over 1,300 banks closed

1931 Bank panic

1931 Unemployment on the rise

1932 Franklin Roosevelt elected president

1932 New Deal legislation passed during first 100 days

1933 Bank holiday declared

1933 AAA, CCC, TVA, NIRA passed

1933 Prohibition repealed by Twenty-first Amendment

1935 WPA created; Social Security Act passed

1935 NIRA declared unconstitutional

1936 FDR reelected in a landslide

1937 Court "packing" plan defeated

1937 National Labor Relations Act passed

1938 Country faces economic recession

1939 World War II begins; United States remains neutral

1940 FDR elected to third term

1940 Selective Service Act passed

1940 Lend-Lease program begins

1941 Pearl Harbor attacked; United States enters the war

1941 Four Freedoms introduced by FDR

1942 United States loses major Pacific battles

1942 Japanese-American internment begins

1944 Tide turns in favor of the Allies

1944 FDR reelected to a fourth term

1945 Yalta and Potsdam conferences

1945 FDR dies in office; Truman becomes new president

1945 Atomic bomb dropped; WW II ends

During the 1932 election, Franklin Delano Roosevelt promised the American people a New Deal. Suggesting to the public that "the only thing we have to fear is fear itself," FDR embarked on an ambitious program during his first 100 days to accomplish the goals of the New Deal—relief, recovery, and reform.

CAUSES OF THE GREAT DEPRESSION

CHAPTER FLASHBACK:

The roots of the causes of the Great Depression took place during the Roaring Twenties. Prosperity took hold and a new middle class enjoyed the fruits of it.

"Black Tuesday"

The stock market was booming, until 1929 when the single largest drop in stock market history occurred. Overspeculation of stocks was the chief cause. Read the following Eyewitness Account of a stockbroker on the floor of the Exchange on what was called "Black Tuesday."

SHERLOCK EYEWITNESS ACCOUNT:

They roared like a lot of lions and tigers. They hollered and screamed, they clawed at one another's collars. It was like a bunch of crazy men. Every once in a while, when Radio or Steel or Auburn would take another tumble, you'd see some poor devil collapse and fall to the floor.

Forty percent of the value of stock was wiped out. By 1933 the market's value was 20 percent lower than at its peak in 1929. Businesses shut down, unemployment increased to almost 25 percent of the work force, banks failed, farmers' profits declined by almost 50 percent, and a new expression was born–the Great Depression. Unfortunately for Herbert Hoover, he was the president who had to deal with the worst economic crisis in American history.

HISTORICAL TIDBIT:

It is commonly believed that the Roaring Twenties was a period of prosperity for most Americans. In fact, by the end of the decade, close to 60 percent of American families were living in poverty.

Hoover could not get the country out of the depression, even though he did pursue what has been called "trickle-down economics":

- cutting taxes that he hoped would spur the public to buy goods
- spending government money on public projects such as dams, highways, and harbors
- getting Congress to pass the Reconstruction Finance Corporation, which gave federal funds to banks in trouble and other industries that were threatened by bankruptcy
- ordering a stop to war payment debts in order to halt the worldwide spread of the depression

These measures failed, and a new politician came on the scene with a new vision. Franklin Delano Roosevelt, governor of New York, was nominated by the Democrats and ran against Hoover in the 1932 election. Because the country was in the midst of the depression, the results were a foregone conclusion: Roosevelt won in what was described as a landslide; he received 472 electoral votes to Hoover's 59 votes.

HISTORICAL TIDBIT:

Roosevelt used as his campaign theme song "Happy Days Are Here Again." It came from a movie called *Chasing Rainbows*. The movie got terrible reviews but the song will always be identified with Roosevelt's successful campaign.

Roosevelt had a name for his plan. He called it a "New Deal for the American People." Unlike Hoover, he believed it was the responsibility of the federal government to solve the problems facing the country. Immediately following his inauguration, he started addressing the problems during the first 100 days of his new administration.

FDR'S FIRST 100 DAYS

Utilizing the mass media in the form of "fireside chats" broadcast on radio, he attempted to calm the American people. One of his first acts was to call a bank holiday in order to stop the panic of the public who were lining up to get their money out of banks before they failed. Other measures during the first 100 days included insuring bank deposits, paying farmers to stop growing crops, asking businesses to establish fair prices, getting Congress to pass a minimum wage, and establishing a forty-hour work week.

F. D. ROOSEVELT

Let's look at an excerpt from one of FDR's fireside chats:

> *By the afternoon of March 3 scarcely a bank in the country was open to do business. Proclamations temporarily closing them in whole or in part had been issued by the Governors in almost all the states.*
>
> *It was then that I issued the proclamation providing for the nation-wide bank holiday, and this was the first step in the Government's reconstruction of our financial and economic fabric.*

What motivated Roosevelt to declare this holiday? Do you think it was a good idea? What would you have done if you were facing economic hardship and had money in the bank?

Because there was such a panic, Roosevelt had no choice but to ask the banks not to open for the time being. Using his fireside chat, which he gave over the radio, he calmed the people, and shortly thereafter the banks reopened.

Even though these early efforts were made to take action to deal with the depression, the fact remained that most people were suffering. **Bread lines** were a common sight. Homeless people were sleeping on the streets and the number one song of the period was "Brother, Can You Spare a Dime."

Bread line—People lined up to get food at government sponsored locations.

Let's take a look at an eyewitness account of what it was like living during the Great Depression from Library of Congress web site "The Federal Writers Project."

Why was this period called the Great Depression?

> *I never dreamed it would last until my shelves were empty and my drawing account dwindled. Still hoping against hope I kept on buying and selling on credit until my last dollar was gone. I had $6,000 in diamonds; one ring alone was worth $3,300. I sold all of them with the exception of my engagement and wedding rings.*

Source: *I Am Reaping in Tears What I Sowed in Fun, A Depression Victim Story.* Leila H. Harris, Supervising Editor. Georgia Writers' Project, Area 7.

The eyewitness accounts provide firsthand experiences of people living during the Great Depression. They illustrate the extent to which people lost their life's earnings. Why not try interviewing your grandparents, if they lived during this time, and see what they remember about it?

THE NEW DEAL

```
                        ┌──────────────────┐
                        │   The New Deal   │
                        └──────────────────┘
                 ↙              ↓              ↘
    ┌──────────────┐  ┌──────────────┐  ┌──────────────┐
    │    Relief    │  │   Recovery   │  │    Reform    │
    └──────────────┘  └──────────────┘  └──────────────┘
           ↓                 ↓                 ↓
```

Relief	Recovery	Reform
Federal Emergency Relief Administration	Agricultural Adjustment Act (AAA)	Federal Deposit Insurance Corporation (FDIC)
Public Works Administration (PWA)	National Recovery Administration	Securities and Exchange Commission
Civilian Conservation Corps (CCC)		National Labor Relations Board (NLRB)
Works Progress Administration (WPA)		

New Deal legislation

Relief for the Poor and Unemployed:

Federal Emergency Relief Administration (FERA) (1933). It gave federal money to the states, which in turn gave money to people in need.

Public Works Administration (PWA) (1933). Federal government money was used to create jobs for the purpose of building new highways, bridges, and dams.

Civilian Conservation Corps (CCC) (1933). This created jobs for young people in the area of environmental protection.

Works Progress Administration (WPA) (1935). It put unemployed workers back on the job by creating special federal jobs, such as repairing schools and roads.

Recovery of Business, Housing, and Agriculture:

Agricultural Adjustment Act (AAA) (1933). This act subsidized farmers after they destroyed crops and limited production.

National Recovery Administration (NRA) (1933). It created executive power to set standards for businesses utilizing the National Industrial Recovery Board.

These two acts were later declared unconstitutional by the Supreme Court. As a result, Roosevelt attempted to **pack** the Supreme Court with additional justices. Congress refused to go along with his plan.

Court packing—Plan favored by Franklin Roosevelt after two of his New Deal programs were ruled unconstitutional. He wanted Congress to expand the size of the Supreme Court. They refused.

HISTORICAL TIDBIT:

The court packing idea was originally proposed by one of the justices Roosevelt wanted to replace.

Federal Housing Administration (FHA). This allowed for the recovery of the housing industry in the form of government loans for housing construction.

Reform of the Banking Establishment, Labor, Stock Market, and Senior Citizens in Need:

Federal Deposit Insurance Corporation (FDIC) (1933). This was created by the Glass-Steagall Banking Act and it insured money in banks up to $100,000.

Securities and Exchange Commission (SEC) (1934). This group regulated the stock market and was created to make sure that the speculation that caused the 1929 crash would never happen again.

Social Security Board (SSB) 1934. This was created as a result of the passage of the Social Security Act, giving insurance benefits to the elderly and guaranteeing them an income.

National Labor Relations Board (NLRB) (1935). The Board was created as a result of the National Labor Relations Act, guaranteeing the right of workers to organize.

Congress also created the **Tennessee Valley Authority**, which was given money to provide electricity and build dams and reservoirs.

As you can see, the New Deal attempted to solve the nation's problems. One segment of the society that had suffered because of the weather was the farmers who lived in what was called the "Dust Bowl."

SHERLOCK EYEWITNESS ACCOUNT: LETTER FROM OKLAHOMA WOMAN DESCRIBING DUST BOWL:

In the dust-covered desolation of our No Man's Land here, wearing our shade hats, with handkerchiefs tied over our faces and vaseline in our nostrils, we have been trying to rescue our home from the wind-blown dust which penetrates wherever air can go. It is almost a hopeless task, for there is rarely a day when at some time the dust clouds do not roll over. "Visibility" approaches zero and everything is covered again with a silt-like deposit which may vary in depth from a film to actual ripples on the kitchen floor.

Sherlock's **Question:** Have you ever experienced a weather event that changed your life?

The impact of the New Deal

The legacy of the New Deal has many ironies. Though FDR's plan began moving the country out of the Depression, by 1937 the country was back in an economic recession, forcing the Congress and President Roosevelt to resume heavy federal spending in 1938. It was not until our involvement in World War II that the country had full employment and came completely out of the Great Depression. The lasting impact of the New Deal can still be felt in today's society as many of the New Deal programs such as the TVA, Social Security, and FDIC still exist.

Let's compare prices during the depression with prices of similar items today.

Here is an example of one of the categories:

Then and Now: Wages (weekly averages)

Job	Then	Now
Manufacturing—Production Worker	$16.89	$500
Cook	$15.00	$236
Doctor	$61.11	$1,800
Accountant	$45.00	$700

Looking at the chart, it should be obvious why the period led to so much suffering. The comparison of prices and wages is staggering. Can you think of any other prices that have changed dramatically during your lifetime?

WORLD WAR II

From isolation to involvement

Ironically, the period called the Great Depression really ended with the outbreak of World War II. When a country enters a war, its entire economy shifts, production gears up to help fight the war, employment increases, and, as a result, the economy prospers. That's exactly what happened when the United States entered World War II. Why did we move from an official policy of neutrality after the war broke out in Europe in 1939? Two words: Pearl Harbor.

The presidential election of 1940 was a turning point for Franklin Roosevelt. His decision to run for a third term broke the long-standing tradition set by George Washington. The American people responded and his victory over Republican Wendell Willkie was also a victory against those people who were known as *isolationists*, arguing that under no circumstances should the United States get involved in the problems facing Europe.

After his election, Congress passed the Lend-Lease Act, which allowed Roosevelt to transfer arms and equipment to Great Britain, the Soviet Union, and China, which the president felt was important to the security of the United States. This act angered Germany and Japan. By the fall of 1941, with the Nazis conquering most of Europe and Japan expanding its empire in Asia, our relations with Japan had deteriorated. Roosevelt ordered all Japanese assets in the United States frozen. Japan was told that if they withdrew from China and Indochina, the United States would release those assets. Roosevelt made a direct appeal to the Japanese emperor Hirohito on December 6, 1941. The next day, Japan responded by attacking our naval base at Pearl Harbor in Hawaii.

HISTORICAL TIDBIT:

The Japanese Naval Academy asked its students as part of their final exam to write an essay describing how they would plan a surprise attack on Pearl Harbor.

After the initial shock of the event, the president asked for a declaration of war from Congress, describing the attack as "a day which will live in infamy [disgrace]." The attack was devastating: Nineteen ships and 150 planes were destroyed; almost 2,500 men of the armed forces and civilians were killed or wounded.

There is a permanent museum in Hawaii at Pearl Harbor and a memorial of the battleship *Arizona,* which was sunk.

SHERLOCK EYEWITNESS ACCOUNT:

A few moments later I found myself deep below the water line in a part of the ship I normally would never be in. I remember getting these cases of ammo powder and shells weighing about 90 pounds each. I had begun lifting shells into the hoist when a deafening roar filled the room and the entire ship shuttered. It was the forward magazine. One and half million pounds of gun powder exploding in a massive fireball disintegrating the whole forward part of the ship. Only moments before I stood with my gun crew just a few feet from the center of the explosion. Admiral Kidd, Captain Van Velkenburg, my whole gun crew was killed. Everyone on top.

—George D. Phraner, Aviation Machinists Mate 1/c, U.S.S. *Arizona* (BB-39), Battle Station; Forward 5 inch Gun

Sherlock Question: Why was the attack on Pearl Harbor called a "sneak attack"?

The home front

Once war broke out, the United States mobilized. We committed the production of:

- 60,000 planes
- 45,000 tanks
- 20,000 anti-aircraft guns

The entire economy from farming to manufacturing, banking, and labor agreed to the goal of defeating the axis powers of Japan, Germany, and Italy. Though there was rationing of consumer goods, the country was united in its determination to defeat the aggressors in a two-front war–in Europe and in Asia.

Because the armed forces increased its numbers through a military draft, for the first time women became actively involved in wartime production. The nickname "Rosie the Riveter" was given to these women and the following poster proclaimed Rosie's involvement.

"Rosie the Riveter" illustrates how women as young as 14 or 15 worked in factories. The poster you see helped give women pride in what they were doing.

The government also rallied the home front through a series of wartime posters that can be viewed as **propaganda**.

Propaganda–The spreading of ideas and information by the government to convince the American people they should unite in the war effort.

Look at the following wartime posters from the National Archives. How do these posters reflect government propaganda? How do they portray the Nazis and Japanese?

These propaganda posters and others found at the National Archives vividly portray the efforts of the

government to get the undivided support of the American people. In using the word "United," the "United We Stand" poster has a second message that both blacks and whites are working together. The "Warning" poster portrays in almost cartoon form what the enemy looks like, and has the side effect of using fear to get citizens behind the government.

The internment of Japanese-Americans

Along with the attempts to unify the home front, the government was also concerned about the threat of Japanese spies, especially on the West Coast. In 1942 Roosevelt agreed to issue an executive order that placed Japanese-Americans in internment camps for the duration of the war.

SHERLOCK EYEWITNESS ACCOUNT: FIRSTHAND ACCOUNT OF JAPANESE INTERNMENT:

I would want everyone to know that all of us, the American citizens born in this country as well as our grandparents and parents who originally came from Japan were innocent of any wrong. We were loyal Americans. The FBI and military investigated all persons of Japanese ancestry and found we were loyal Americans. There was no single incident of any hint of treason or wrong. A typical day in an internment camp such as Jerome would begin with families getting up. Remember we did not have any water in our rooms. We just had one light bulb and a small stove. We had to get dressed and go to the middle of the block to use the toilet, wash up and take showers. Usually there were people waiting in lines. After you brushed your teeth and cleaned up, you had to go to a separate building for breakfast, lunch, and dinner. They had two sessions. If you were late or forgot your ticket, you could not eat. We stood in line for the food, which was served on metal trays, and we sat at long wooden tables with benches. There really wasn't much to do the rest of the time. . . . We didn't have TV in those days. And we did not have a radio.

—Marielle Tsukamoto

Do you think this was a reasonable policy? Find out what the government did after new evidence emerged about Japanese-Americans during the 1980s.

As you read the sad story of how and why the government made the decision to put Japanese-American citizens behind barbed wire, you should be struck by the conflicting reasons the government gave. On the one hand, during a time of war a government has the obligation to protect its citizens, even if it means limiting civil liberties. On the other hand, the government must prove there is a real threat. Roosevelt knew that the Japanese living on the West Coast did not present this kind of threat and agreed to the policy for political reasons. In 1988 the government apologized, and gave $20,000 to Japanese survivors of these camps.

The Holocaust

While Japanese-Americans were kept behind barbed wire, a far worse fate befell millions of people in Europe. The Germans systematically killed six million Jews and millions of other minorities in what is known as the Holocaust.

The role of the United States has been chronicled at the Holocaust Museum in Washington, D.C. Visit it on-line at:

http://www.ushmm.org/

Write down your feelings about the Holocaust. Do you think the United States could have done more to stop the atrocities?

Visiting the United States Holocaust Museum is a very emotional experience. The Internet site gives you a flavor and information about the museum and the terrible events of the Holocaust. Even though the United States knew what was going on, nothing was done militarily to stop the atrocities. In addition, when he had the opportunity to aid a refugee ship, the *St. Louis*, President Roosevelt refused to grant these immigrants a safe haven in America because there were immigration restrictions. The ship returned to Europe where most of the passengers ended up in German concentration camps.

The battle lines

The war on the battlefield was brutal. Along with our allies, Great Britain, France, and eventually the Soviet Union, we had to defeat the Nazis in Europe and the Japanese in Asia. Both efforts cost the lives of thousands of American soldiers. The wartime strategy was plotted by President Roosevelt,

British Prime Minister Winston Churchill, and Soviet leader Joseph Stalin, in a series of wartime summit meetings:

- **Newfoundland, Canada** (August, 1941)—Prior to our official involvement in the war, Roosevelt and Churchill issued the Atlantic Charter, a statement that outlined our mutual objectives. Roosevelt promised the American people four freedoms—freedom from war, freedom from fear, freedom from want, and freedom of the seas.
- **Casablanca, Morocco** (January, 1943)—The policy of "unconditional surrender," stating that Germany would have to surrender without any conditions, was announced.
- **Cairo, Egypt** (1943)—Roosevelt and Churchill, along with the Chinese leader Chiang Kai-shek, agreed that Japan would have to return all conquered lands.
- **Tehran, Iran** (1943)—A new international organization to be called the United Nations was agreed upon.
- **Yalta, Soviet Union**, and **Potsdam, Germany** (1945)—The United States, England, and the Soviet Union met at Yalta and Potsdam and started making postwar plans. These included an agreement for the Soviets to enter the war after the defeat of Germany and an agreement that would allow more Soviet influence in Eastern Europe, an opening that would eventually mean Communist domination over that area.

As for the war itself, there were many key battles.

Significant Battles of World War II

Pearl Harbor
Blitzkrieg in the West
The Fall of France
Battle of Britain
The Siege of Leningrad
Bataan and Corregidor
Guadalcanal
The Battle of Stalingrad
Liberation of Italy
North Africa and Sicily
Battle for the Philippines

D-Day–The Beginning of the End
Atom Bombs dropped on Japan

 HISTORICAL TIDBIT:

World War II was the most expensive war in
American history, costing over $550 billion.
Did you know that the "D" in D-day, according to army
sources, stood for "date" not "decision"?

 **SHERLOCK EYEWITNESS ACCOUNT**

*Lieutenant McBride, Captain Slater, and
one-third of our company went down as
their boat swamped. We landed and fired
off our rockets, the ramp goes down, and
I'm the first guy shot in the company, a
machine gun through the right side. Then I stepped off
into water over my head, and the guys pulled me out and
we just rushed to the base of that cliff and grabbed any
rope we could get, and up the cliff we went just as fast as
we could go. The wound wasn't bad; it had gone through
the muscle on my right side.*

—Leonard Lomell

Sherlock's Question: How did D-day change the course of
World War II?

The end of the war

After the war ended in Europe
in 1945, a difficult decision had
to be made. What was the best
and fastest way to end the war
in Asia? Unfortunately for this
country, President Roosevelt,
who had just been re-elected to an
unprecedented fourth term, died

in April of a cerebral hemorrhage. The new president, Harry Truman, was presented with the information that a new weapon, the atomic bomb, had been developed by a group of scientists working on what was called the Manhattan Project.

What is your view regarding the morality of using weapons of destruction, even though in the end it brought a quick resolution to the war?

The decision to drop the bomb had to be a most difficult one, especially for a new president who had not even been aware that such a weapon existed. Without a doubt, an invasion of Japan would have resulted in major casualties for the United States. We learned in the war that Japan believed that surrender was not an option. Kamikaze pilots took on suicide missions and attacked our navy. Yet survivors still feel the effects of the bomb, and the bomb did usher in a new era—the Atomic Age.

FDR'S LEGACY

Before Sherlock leaves this era of American history, we should look more closely at the importance of Roosevelt's presidency. Most historians rank him as one of our top five presidents. A memorial was built in his honor at Washington, D.C.'s Mall. His wife Eleanor also has been recognized as one of the most influential First Ladies.

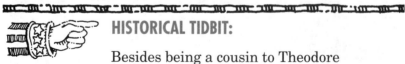

HISTORICAL TIDBIT:

Besides being a cousin to Theodore Roosevelt, Franklin was also related to ten other presidents.

Do you agree with the view of the historians who rank FDR as one of the great presidents?

Because the country went through two of the most traumatic events in its history—the Great Depression and World War II—and the Roosevelts were the occupants of the White House during this time, they are believed to have provided the leadership the country needed at the time.

SHERLOCK'S MATCHING MADNESS: THE NEW DEAL

Match the New Deal program with its purpose.

Federal Emergency Relief Administration	Gave insurance benefits to the elderly
Public Works Administration	Guaranteed the right of workers to organize
Civilian Conservation Corps	Provided electricity, dams, and reservoirs
Works Progress Administration	Gave to the states federal money, which helped people in need
Social Security	Used federal money to provide jobs for the purpose of building new highways
National Labor Relations Act	Created jobs for young people in the area of environmental protection
Tennessee Valley Authority	Put unemployed workers back on the job

CHAPTER TEN

Postwar America
(1946-1968)

THE BERLIN WALL FROM WEST BERLIN

Ask not what your country can do for you—ask what you can do for your country.
                    —John F. Kennedy, Inaugural Address, 1961

Time Line (1946–1968)

1946 United Nations General Assembly met for the first time

1947 Truman Doctrine

1947 Marshall Plan adopted

1948 Berlin airlift

1948 Truman reelected president

1949 North Atlantic Treaty Organization (NATO) formed

1950 Korean War begins

1952 Dwight D. Eisenhower elected president

1953 Korean War ends

1953 Cold War spies Julius and Ethel Rosenberg executed

1954 Army-McCarthy hearings

1954 *Brown v. Board of Education* decision ends school segregation

1955 Southeast Asia Treaty Organization (SEATO) formed

1955 Bus boycott in Montgomery, Alabama

1956 Dwight Eisenhower reelected president

1957 Soviet Union launches *Sputnik*

1957 Eisenhower Doctrine announced

1959 Alaska and Hawaii admitted as states

1960 John F. Kennedy elected president

1961 Alan B. Shepard, Jr. first American in space

1961 Bay of Pigs invasion fails

1961 Berlin Wall built

1962 John Glenn first U.S. astronaut to orbit earth

1962 Cuban Missile crisis

1963 Civil Rights advocates marched on Washington

1963 John F. Kennedy assassinated

1963 Lyndon B. Johnson becomes president

1964 Lyndon B. Johnson elected president

1964 Great Society program announced

1965 First combat troops sent to Vietnam

1966 Vietnam War escalates

1967 Thurgood Marshall named first black Supreme Court justice

1968 Antiwar demonstrations on the rise

1968 Johnson announced he wouldn't run for re-election

1968 Martin Luther King, Jr. assassinated

THE COLD WAR

Postwar America struggled to balance its priorities. On the international front, a new kind of war began—the **Cold War**.

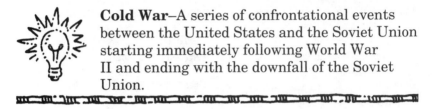

Cold War–A series of confrontational events between the United States and the Soviet Union starting immediately following World War II and ending with the downfall of the Soviet Union.

On the domestic front the country faced the problem of retraining the soldiers who returned from battle. **Sherlock** will take you on a journey of the foreign and domestic polices of the United States from 1946 to 1968. As you look at the Time Line accompanying this chapter, you will notice the period is dominated by four presidents—Harry Truman, Dwight Eisenhower, John Kennedy, and Lyndon Johnson. Part of the story of America is also the story of these leaders.

CHAPTER FLASHBACK:

After the dropping of the atomic bomb and the surrender of Japan, the allied nations of the United States, Great Britain, France, and the Soviet Union put into effect the agreements reached at Yalta and Potsdam. Each country occupied a segment of Germany. The United States, under the leadership of Douglas MacArthur, took on the responsibility of supervising the defeated country of Japan. But the greater problem of what to do to ensure a lasting peace was raised.

Formation of the United Nations

Remember that after World War I the United States refused to participate in the League of Nations. This time it would be different. A new international organization was born in San Fransisco in 1945—the United Nations. Dedicated to maintaining world security, the organization was composed of a General Assembly, made up of all the officially recognized nations of the world, which decided on general policy for the United Nations. There was also the Security Council, consisting of the permanent members of France, the Soviet Union, Great Britain, China, and the United States, each having veto power. The Council also had six other rotating member-nations. The Security Council was responsible for making decisions regarding international disputes.

The United Nations has been on the forefront of trying to settle international disputes since its inception, and, in addition, it has been involved in humanitarian efforts.

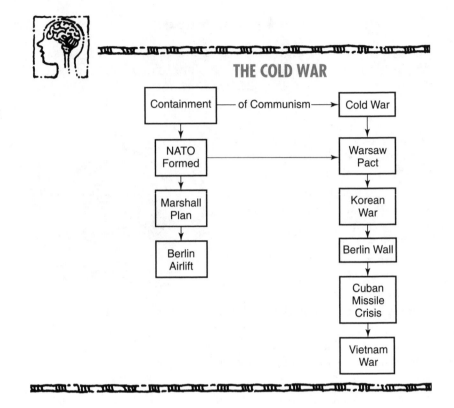

THE COLD WAR

Containment —— of Communism ——→ Cold War

NATO Formed ——————————→ Warsaw Pact

Marshall Plan

Berlin Airlift

Korean War

Berlin Wall

Cuban Missile Crisis

Vietnam War

The early years

Look at the Mind Map and come up with an explanation of the meaning of the Cold War by following the "Containment" arrows and the "Cold War" arrows.

The formula *Containment of Communism = Cold War* is a simple way to understand what the Cold War was all about. As we proceed through our journey, you will clearly see how the containment boxes all were attempts to stop the spread of communism, and you will see how the Cold War events were, to a large extent, a response to those efforts.

President Truman realized that even with a United Nations there would be serious problems in our relations with the Soviet Union. Soon it became evident that the Soviets were intent on maintaining its influence in Eastern Europe as it set up what was called **satellite nations**.

Satellite nations—Those countries in Eastern Europe that had Communist governments imposed on them by the Soviet Union in an effort to make sure they would side with Russia.

Winston Churchill, the prime minister of England, called it an *iron curtain* in a speech where he said,

From Stettin in the Baltic to Trieste in the Adriatic, an iron curtain has descended across the Continent.

SHERLOCK MAP CHALLENGE

Look on the map and find the area that Churchill was referring to.

The Cold War became the longest struggle in United States history. It resulted in an arms buildup that could have easily destroyed the world as we know it. A nuclear nightmare was imagined.

207

The nuclear arms race became the driving force behind the Cold War. Each side felt it must have nuclear superiority over the other. Why do you suppose it was necessary to have an arms race with the Soviet Union when it would take just a few bombs from each side to destroy the planet's environment?

More often than not, the United States was at the brink of war with the Soviet Union during the time of the Cold War, and, in fact, we were in a shooting war in both Korea and Vietnam. The aim of our foreign policy was simple—to make sure communism would not spread.

TRUMAN AND THE COLD WAR

After the iron curtain descended on Eastern Europe, President Truman initiated a number of actions that he felt would stop the spread of communism.

The Truman Doctrine (1947)

This policy provided aid and support to stop the spread of communism in Greece and Turkey.

The Adoption of the Marshall Plan (1947)

Developed by Secretary of State George Marshall, it gave massive aid to Western Europe.

The Berlin Airlift (1948)

In response to the Soviet Union's attempt to blockade the western part of the German capital, which was located deep in the territory of East Germany, the United States for over a year dropped supplies through an airlift.

The Formation of the North Atlantic Treaty Organization (NATO) 1949

NATO is called a collective security agreement, meaning that the United States proclaimed that an attack on any country that was part of NATO would be considered an attack on the United States. The Soviet Union responded by forming the Warsaw Pact, a collective security agreement among the satellite countries of Eastern Europe and the Soviet Union.

These events were very successful in sending a message to the Soviet Union, specifically the Marshall Plan, with its millions of dollars of aid revitalizing Western Europe. The Berlin airlift prevented the Soviet Union from taking over West Berlin, thus preserving it as the capital of Germany. Even today, the United States views NATO as an important deterrent to aggression. In fact, an expansion of the organization in 1998 to include three former Communist Eastern European nations, Poland, Hungary, and the Czech Republic (part of the former Czechoslovakia), was approved.

The Korean War

After the Communists succeeded in overthrowing the democratic government in China in 1949, President Truman concluded that they too would be a potential threat to world peace. By 1950, in the bordering nation of Korea, the prediction came true. As part of the peace agreement ending World War II, Korea was split at the 38th parallel into Communist North Korea and Democratic South Korea. The North was supported by the Soviet Union and China, while the United States supported the South.

In December 1950, North Korean troops crossed the 38th parallel and the first shooting war of the postwar period began. Quickly, the United Nations (without the presence of the Soviet Union, which was protesting the fact that the new Communist Chinese government was not part of the Security Council) approved an "international police force." Without a formal declaration of war, the United States, under the command of General Douglas MacArthur, sent the most troops. At a crucial point during the war, MacArthur challenged President Truman's orders not to expand the war and he was dismissed by the president. The war finally ended in 1953 after a new president, Dwight Eisenhower, was elected. The peace agreement maintained two Koreas and a demilitarized zone at the 38th parallel.

SHERLOCK EYEWITNESS ACCOUNT:

In 1948 President Harry Truman integrated the United States military. The Korean War was the first armed conflict in which African-American soldiers fought side by side with white soldiers. The following is an excerpt from an interview with Air Force Air Controller Robert Gates.

Because the military is a structured system controlled by rank and discipline it is really difficult to compare any racial differences. First of all, because I was in the military I did not get to observe so-called real world happenings. Perhaps due to my youthful age, that is, my leisure time was spent drinking beer, chasing girls and what have you. Also as I have mentioned on a couple of other occasions, I was not raised to be aware of cultural differences and so had no experience along those lines. My parents moved us to Virginia when I had less than two years left of High School. Of course, in Virginia segregation was the rule of the day at that time. But again, it sailed by me because I just didn't devote my attention to it. When I entered the Air Force was just about the time that President Truman ordered integration within the services and the Air Force seemed to tackle the problem in a more agressive manner. So, I am told and everybody was more concerned about rank and its privileges then it was to any cultural or racial situations. I do know for a fact that there existed then and for the next 20 years of my service time that blacks and whites found their off base entertainment in a segregated manner. And within the service it was not uncommon to see blacks congregate together at sports activities, etc. Again, I didn't pay much attention to it and neither did I join in nor was I ever invited to do so.

Sherlock's Question: What was Gates's attitude toward integration of the military?

Because we were hampered by the threat of a larger war if China and the Soviet Union got involved, the eventual peace settlement kept the status quo.

Truman's legacy

No discussion of the early years of the Cold War would be complete without looking more closely at the presidency of Harry Truman. Sworn in after the death of Franklin Roosevelt in 1945, Truman immediately was faced with the difficult decision of whether to drop the atomic bomb. He ran an uphill campaign for re-election in 1948, and surprised the political analysts by coming from behind and defeating New York's governor Thomas Dewey. As president he developed the Cold War strategy we just explored and came up with a domestic policy called "The Fair Deal," which emphasized aid to returning soldiers in the form of a GI Bill. He stood up to striking steelworkers even though the Supreme Court ruled he went too far.

 HISTORICAL TIDBIT:

The Chicago Sun-Times in a banner headline declared: "DEWEY DEFEATS TRUMAN" in its early edition. Truman holds up a copy of it during his victory celebration.

EISENHOWER AND THE COLD WAR

President Dwight D. Eisenhower was elected president of the United States in 1952 using the campaign theme "I Like Ike." He was a grandfather figure for many people and had the status of having been the former Supreme Commander of the Allied Forces during World War II. He promised the country he would end the Korean War, and after his election the peace settlement was secured. During his two terms as president, the country was going through cultural changes as well as continuing its fight against communism.

Sherlock will be focusing on the key themes and events of Eisenhower's administration and visiting related web sites to help you get a picture of what problems Americans were facing.

The Red Scare

Just as the country faced a reaction after Russia turned Communist in 1918, it also did so during the 1950s. Wisconsin senator Joseph McCarthy held hearings to investigate whether there was Communist infiltration in the government. These hearings were given more credibility since two American citizens, Ethel and Julius Rosenberg, were convicted of espionage for turning over nuclear secrets to the Soviet Union and executed in 1953 for that crime.

SHERLOCK DOCUMENT CHALLENGE:

On the day of their execution, Ethel and Julius Rosenberg wrote the following letter to their children:

Dearest Sweethearts, my most precious children,

Only this morning it looked like we might be together again after all. Now that this cannot be, I want so much for you to know all that I have come to know. Unfortunately, I may write only a few simple words; the rest your own lives must teach you, even as mine taught me.

At first, of course, you will grieve bitterly for us, but you will not grieve alone. That is our consolation and it must eventually be yours.

Eventually, too you must come to believe that life is worth the living. Be comforted that even now, with the end of ours slowly approaching, that we know this with a conviction that defeats the executioner!

Your lives must teach you, too, that good cannot flourish in the midst of evil; that freedom and all the things that go to make up a truly satisfying and worthwhile life,

*must sometime be purchased very dearly. Be comforted
then that we were serene and understood with the deepest
kind of understanding, that civilization had not as yet
progressed to the point where life did not have to be lost
for the sake of life; and that we were comforted in the sure
knowledge that others would carry on after us.*

*We wish we might have had the tremendous joy and
gratification of living our lives out with you. Your Daddy
who is with me in the last momentous hours, sends his
heart and all the love that is in it for his dearest boys.
Always remember that we were innocent and could not
wrong our conscience.*

We press you close and kiss you with all our strength.

Lovingly,

Daddy and Mommy
Julie   Ethel

Sherlock's Question: Why do you think there was such
outrage at their conviction and execution?

In fact, many of the individuals called before McCarthy's
committee were *blacklisted*, prevented from working, and
there really was no evidence they were ever involved with
the Communist party because these witnesses took the Fifth
Amendment by refusing to answer the questions asked, based
on the fact they had a right to refuse to incriminate themselves.

The Culture of the 1950s

One of the biggest changes during the presidencies of
Truman and Eisenhower was the birth of the *baby boomers*,
those children born after World War II. The society became
one that was characterized by the growth of the suburbs,
an increase in the use of automobiles, and the appearance
of new leisure activities—television and a new music called
rock and roll.

As a teenager growing up, you have developed your own
cultural interests—favorite TV shows, favorite musical
groups, favorite songs; it was the same for teenagers in the
1950s. Elvis was king and the television age ushered in
new programs such as "I Love Lucy" and the "Howdy Doody

Show." See if your parents or grandparents remember these shows and ask them to tell you more about them.

Civil Rights during Eisenhower's Administration

The 1950s brought about a turning point in the struggle for civil rights. It started with Truman's decision to integrate the military and to end discrimination in federal hiring practices. Then, a recognition that black Americans did not have the full benefit of what the Constitution stated as "equal protection under the law" caused the beginning of what is called the *civil rights revolution*.

Let's trace some of the key political and social events devoted to this theme.

- **The integration of baseball.** Jackie Robinson became the first African-American to break the color barrier in 1947.

  The right of every American to first-class citizenship is the most important issue of our time.

  I don't think that I or any other Negro, as an American citizen, should have to ask for anything that is rightfully his. We are demanding that we just be given the things that are rightfully ours and that we're not looking for anything else.

  —Jackie Robinson

- How did Robinson impact the civil rights movement?
- As much as any political leader, Jackie Robinson's successful baseball career made him a role model.
- **The political movement to end desegregation.** Since the Supreme Court ruled in 1896 in a very famous case, *Plessy v. Ferguson,* that the doctrine called "separate but equal" was legal, segregation became a legal way to keep the races separated.

  By the 1950s The National Association for the Advancement of Colored People (NAACP), led by attorney, and later the first African-American Supreme Court justice, Thurgood Marshall, began a legal challenge. The case became known as *Brown v. Topeka Board of Education* and it was argued in 1954.

It involved a black elementary student, Linda Brown, who was not allowed to attend a white school nearest to her house. Marshall successfully argued that her equal protection rights found in the Fourteenth Amendment were violated. The Supreme Court ruled unanimously that segregation in schools was illegal.

The following is an excerpt from the Supreme Court unanimous decision written by Chief Justice Earl Warren:

We come then to the question presented: Does segregation of children in public schools solely on the basis of race, even though the physical facilities and other "tangible" factors may be equal, deprive the children of the minority group of equal educational opportunities? We believe that it does . . . We conclude that in the field of public education the doctrine of "separate but equal" has no place. Separate educational facilities are inherently unequal. Therefore, we hold that the plaintiffs and others similarly situated for whom the actions have been brought are, by reason of the segregation complained of, deprived of the equal protection of the laws guaranteed by the Fourteenth Amendment.

Sherlock's Question: What does the phrase "separate educational facilities are inherently unequal" mean?

This case was one of the most important cases the Supreme Court has ever decided. The emotional arguments made by Marshall included a sociological study. This survey, conducted by sociologist Kenneth Clark, asked black students to select their favorite doll. They were given a choice between a white doll and black doll. Most of the children selected the white doll because they indicated they felt inferior.

BIOGRAPHY SPOTLIGHT: DWIGHT D. EISENHOWER:

- Thirty-fourth President of the United States
- **July 27, 1953:** The 38th parallel is established between North and South Korea.
- **December 8, 1953:** Proposition for an International Atomic Energy Agency and peaceful development of Nuclear Energy.
- **June 29, 1956:** Signed Federal Highway Bill creating the Interstate Highway System.
- **September 9, 1957:** Signed the Civil Rights Act, which seeks to protect voting rights.
- **January 31, 1958:** *Explorer 1* went into orbit, becoming America's first satellite.
- **July 29, 1958:** President Eisenhower signed the bill creating NASA.
- **January 3, 1959:** Alaska became the forty-ninth state.
- **April 25, 1959:** St. Lawrence Seaway opened.
- **August 21, 1959:** Hawaii becomes the fiftieth state.
- **November 8, 1060:** Vice President Richard M. Nixon is defeated by Senator John F. Kennedy for President.
- **January 17, 1961:** President Dwight David Eisenhower gives his Farewell Address.

HISTORICAL TIDBIT:

Eisenhower defeated Democratic candidate Adlai Stevenson in both the 1952 and 1956 elections.

A NEW PRESIDENT, A NEW DECADE OF CHANGE

If the fifties was a decade of conformity, the sixties became known as a decade of changes. The election of 1960 certainly presented the voters with a choice of maintaining the status quo or choosing the youngest candidate for president in American history. When Kennedy defeated Eisenhower's vice president Richard Nixon by one of the closest electoral margins, the new president declared that the country was on course to conquer a "New Frontier."

The space race

Domestically, this pledge was carried out in dramatic fashion when the United States began to catch up to the Soviet Union in what became known as the space race. In 1957 the Soviets launched the first orbiting satellite, *Sputnik*. The United States was shocked. A new emphasis was placed on science education, and a high priority was placed on catching up with the Soviets. After Kennedy was elected, he also made a pledge that we would be the first country to set foot on the moon by the end of the decade.

The rest of the Kennedy domestic agenda included:

- the establishment of the **Peace Corps**, whose aim was to send men and women overseas to help developing countries
- the support of **civil rights legislation** and the sending of federal troops to guarantee school integration in the South

The Cold War heats up

The Cold War reached its peak during the Kennedy administration in two areas:

Cuba

Immediately following Kennedy's inauguration, an ill-fated invasion of Cuba, called the "Bay of Pigs invasion," was sponsored by the Central Intelligence Agency (CIA). Because of its failure, the Soviet Union thought it was dealing with a weak president and secretly agreed to begin the process of sending missiles to Cuba. The crisis reached a peak over a period of 14 days in October, 1962. The event became known as the *Cuban Missile Crisis,* and it was the closest the world came to nuclear war.

SHERLOCK ROLE PLAYING:

Take the role of President Kennedy and decide what option you would take.

Source: Kennedy Library National Security Files:

Subject: Policy Toward Non-Bloc Ships in Cuban Trade—Recommended Action

1. The President should make a public statement dealing with this topic.
2. The President should close all U.S. ports to all ships of any country if any ship under the flag of that country hereafter carries arms to Cuba.
3. The President should direct that no government cargo shall be carried on a foreign flag ship if any ship of the same owners is used hereafter in Bloc-Cuba Trade.
4. The President should direct that no U.S. flag ship and no U.S. owned ship shall carry goods to or from Cuba.
5. Alternative I—The President should close all United States ports to any ship on a continuous voyage to or from Cuba.
   Alternative II—The President should close all United States ports to any ship that on the same continuous voyage carried or carries to Cuba items on the COCOM list.
   Alternative III—The President should close all United States ports to any ship that on the same continuous voyage carried or carries to Cuba items on the positive list under Regulation T-1.

Alternative IV—The President should close all United States ports to any ship that on the same continuous voyage was used or is being used in Bloc-Cuba trade.

6. The President should instruct the Secretary of State to explore every avenue to obtain cooperation from other countries in restricting the use of their ships in Bloc-Cuba Trade.

The Cuban Missile Crisis was perhaps the greatest nuclear threat. One false move and the result would have been massive destruction. Interestingly, after the crisis, both sides made an effort to reduce the testing of nuclear bombs in the atmosphere. The result was the first nuclear test ban treaty signed in 1963.

Germany and Berlin Were Still Divided

Between the time of the Bay of Pigs and the Cuban Missile Crisis, Soviet leader Nikita Khrushchev saw another opening to keep communism intact in Berlin. Because of an increasing exodus of people leaving East Berlin, the Soviets 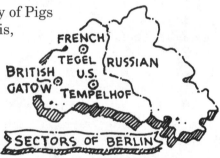 and East Germans built what became known as the *Berlin Wall* in 1961. The wall was an actual physical barrier that separated East Berlin from West Berlin. Until The fall of Communism and the liberation of East Germany in 1989, over five thousand East Germans successfully fled East Berlin by jumping over the barbed wire on the wall. There were also hundreds of unsuccessful attempts, resulting in either the capture of the East Germans, injury, or death. After the wall was built, President John F. Kennedy addressed hundreds of thousands of Germans in West Berlin. He pledged support and in his speech made the now famous statement "Ich bin ein Berliner" (I am a Berliner). In 1987, President Ronald Reagan also addressed throngs of Germans at the Brandenburg Gate in Berlin and said, "Mr. Gorbachev, tear down this wall."

Why does the Wall more than any other event illustrate the real meaning of the Cold War?

As you look at the history of the Berlin Wall, and you think back at Churchill's statement of how communism represented an iron curtain, reflect on how the physical wall around the city, with its barbed wire at the top, represented this kind of image. That's why when the Wall was torn down in 1989, it signaled the official end of the Cold War.

Kennedy's assassination

In November 1963, John F. Kennedy was gunned down in a motorcade by Lee Harvey Oswald in Dallas, Texas. Like the assassination of Lincoln and other presidents before him, this event changed the course of history. Unlike other presidents whose lives were taken, however, Kennedy was the first president whose activities were covered so extensively by the media. There has also been an ongoing controversy over whether or not the assassination was a conspiracy. The National Archives houses the complete records of the assassination. Many web sites deal with this subject.

After President Kennedy was assassinated, President Johnson appointed Supreme Court Chief Justice Earl Warren to head a commission that would investigate the murder of the president. Members of the commission included Gerald Ford, other members of Congress, and the director of the Central Intelligence Agency. The commission held hearings and presented a report that was close to one thousand pages long. There are also many conspiracy theories that disagree with the findings of the government's Warren Commission Report, which concluded that Lee Harvey Oswald was the lone shooter. Ed Hoffman was an eyewitness to the assassination and gave the following account of a shooter he saw on the grassy knoll:

I could see that the top was down on the president's car and I could see the people inside waving at the crowds, although I couldn't make out yet who was who. Part of me wanted to concentrate on seeing the president, but I couldn't keep from looking back at the two men behind the fence.

Just as I did look back, the man in the business suit raised the gun. I saw him rest it on the pickets in the fence. . . .

And just then I saw a spark of light. I saw a puff of fluffy white smoke. The first thing that crossed my mind was that it might be from a cigarette, but it was much too big for that.

When I realized it was a shot, I was totally shocked. I couldn't believe it.

An instant later, I saw the businessman turn back away from the fence, and as he turned around, I could clearly see the gun in his hand. I could see the brown stock as he held the gun out in front of him. Then, very quickly, he tossed the gun over to the train man and started running. He ran past the parked cars and kept on going, running north into the railroad yards.

Just imagine what it must have been like to witness these events live on television.

Kennedy's legacy

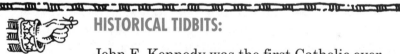

HISTORICAL TIDBITS:

John F. Kennedy was the first Catholic ever to be elected president of the United States. As First Lady, Jackie Kennedy commissioned a historical restoration of the entire White House.

LYNDON B. JOHNSON— A PRESIDENT FACING CRISIS

The presidency of Lyndon Johnson was marked by dramatic programs known as the "Great Society." Yet his decision to escalate the war in Vietnam undermined the great vision and the far-reaching scope of what he had previously accomplished.

Announced to Congress in a dramatic speech after he became president, his intention was to "continue" the goals of the Kennedy administration's New Frontier. He promised to fight for a far-reaching civil rights law and a victory in the form of a "war against poverty."

Johnson accomplished an initial victory in the form of the Economic Opportunity Act of 1964, which authorized one billion dollars of federal money for antipoverty programs.

Martin Luther King, Jr., symbolized the hopes and dreams of African-Americans. His inspirational speeches calling on blacks and whites to become brothers and sisters certainly set in motion the passage of historic civil rights laws.

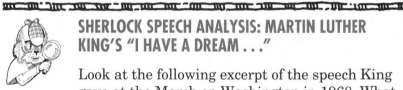

SHERLOCK SPEECH ANALYSIS: MARTIN LUTHER KING'S "I HAVE A DREAM . . ."

Look at the following excerpt of the speech King gave at the March on Washington in 1968. What emotions did King try to appeal to with this speech?

I have a dream that one day this nation will rise up and live out the true meaning of its creed: "We hold these truths to be self-evident, that all men are created equal."

I have a dream that one day on the red hills of Georgia, the sons of former slaves and the sons of former slave owners will be able to sit down together at the table of brotherhood.

I have a dream that one day even the state of Mississippi, a state sweltering with the heat of injustice, sweltering with the heat of oppression, will be transformed into an oasis of freedom and justice.

I have a dream that my four little children will one day live in a nation where they will not be judged by the color of their skin but by the content of their character.

The election of 1964

Setting the stage for new federal programs, Johnson waged a battle against Arizona senator Barry Goldwater in which he portrayed Goldwater as an extremist. In one of the most famous political commercials, a little girl was counting daisies and a voice in the background counted down from ten to zero. At zero, a nuclear bomb exploded.

It was ironic since Johnson's escalation of the war in Vietnam certainly could be described by some as a questionable military move. Johnson won the election by one of the biggest landslides in history and carried with him a large Democratic majority in Congress.

The Great Society

Sherlock looks at some of the Great Society programs signed into law:

- **Elementary and Secondary Education Act.** Its purpose was to provide federal funds for schools with large numbers of children from poor income families. One of its provisions was Head Start, which gave an education to preschool children from lower-income families.
- **Higher Education Act.** This act helped low-income, qualified students to attend college.
- **Housing and Urban Development Act.** This act assisted low-income families in obtaining affordable housing by authorizing 2.9 billion dollars in federal grants for low-rent apartments.
- **Appalachian Development Act.** The purpose of this act was to help rural and depressed regions in Appalachia.
- **Medicare.** Its aim was to help senior citizens pay for medical care after they retired. A second law called **Medicaid** was also passed. This was a form of welfare for seniors who could not afford to pay for Medicare.
- **Civil rights.** In the area of civil rights, two important laws were passed: The Civil Rights Act of 1964, which guaranteed that there would not be any discrimination in public accommodations, such as hotels, and also outlawed discrimination in government facilities and

in federally supported programs, and the Voting Rights Act, which prohibited the practice of using literacy tests to keep African-Americans from voting.

Because Johnson was so successful on the domestic front and literally was forced to make a decision not to run for re-election in 1968 because of the war in Vietnam, his presidency had a dual character.

The Vietnam War

Johnson was convinced that the **domino theory** was more than just a theory.

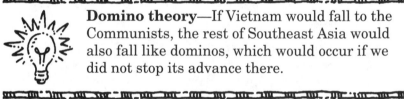

Domino theory—If Vietnam would fall to the Communists, the rest of Southeast Asia would also fall like dominos, which would occur if we did not stop its advance there.

After North Vietnam fired on our ships in international waters, he convinced Congress to pass The Gulf of Tonkin Resolution. It was a turning point in our involvement in Vietnam when, in August 1964, North Vietnamese ships allegedly attacked two U.S. ships. Johnson used this as an excuse to convince Congress to authorize the sending of troops to Vietnam.

SHERLOCK DOCUMENT CHALLENGE: THE GULF OF TONKIN RESOLUTION:

Look at the actual resolution passed by the United States Congress in response to the Gulf of Tonkin incident. What did the resolution accomplish? What was the danger of passing this resolution?

Joint Resolution of Congress
H.J. RES 1145 August 7, 1964

Resolved by the Senate and House of Representatives of the United States of America in Congress assembled,

That the Congress approves and supports the determination of the President, as Commander in Chief, to take all necessary measures to repel any armed attack against the forces of the United States and to prevent further aggression.

Section 2. The United States regards as vital to its national interest and to world peace the maintenance of international peace and security in southeast Asia. Consonant with the Constitution of the United States and the Charter of the United Nations and in accordance with its obligations under the Southeast Asia Collective Defense Treaty, the United States is, therefore, prepared, as the President determines, to take all necessary steps, including the use of armed force, to assist any member or protocol state of the Southeast Asia Collective Defense Treaty requesting assistance in defense of its freedom.

Sometimes history is painful. This is especially true when we later find out that actions regarding an event that took place should not have occurred. We saw this when Roosevelt ordered the internment of Japanese-Americans during World War II, and again, after many years, we saw it in relation to Vietnam. What do you think is the lesson to be learned?

Over a four-year period, LBJ sent in close to 500,000 troops in the largest undeclared war in American history. With the escalation of the war, public opinion turned against Johnson and the Congress was diverted from continuing to pass more Great Society legislation. The turning point came in 1968 when the "Tet offensive" took place. Even though the United States turned back the Viet Cong, public opinion began to go against the president.

There have been many comparisons made between Lyndon Johnson and Franklin Roosevelt. FDR had his New Deal, and Johnson had his Great Society. FDR successfully led the country during World War II, and Johnson was president during the longest war in American history. But that is where the comparison falls flat, as the Vietnam War became the only war in American history that we lost, and it became as much of a legacy for Johnson as the vision he had when he declared that the United States would be turned into a Great Society.

In March 1968, Johnson declared that he would not seek re-election. The election of 1968, and the entire year, became a turning point in American history.

SHERLOCK'S MATCHING MADNESS: THE GREAT SOCIETY:

Match the Great Society program with its goal.

Elementary and Secondary Education Act	Helped rural and depressed areas
Housing and Urban Development Act	Helped senior citizens pay for medical care after they retired
Appalachian Development Act	Provided federal funds for schools and established Head Start
Medicare	Made discrimination in public accommodations illegal
Medicaid	Prohibited the use of literacy tests in elections
Civil Rights Act of 1964	Assisted low-income families in obtaining affordable housing
Voting Rights Act of 1965	Gave poor senior citizens medical assistance

CHAPTER ELEVEN

Modern America
(1968-2000)

RICHARD NIXON
1969-1974

JIMMY CARTER
1977-1981

RONALD
REAGAN
1981-1989

GEORGE H.W.
BUSH
1989-1993

BILL
CLINTON
1993-2001

That's one small step for man, one giant leap for mankind.

—Neil Armstrong, 1969

Time Line (1968–1999)

1968 Robert F. Kennedy assassinated	**1983** Terrorists bomb U.S. marine barracks in Lebanon
1968 Riots at the Democratic National Convention in Chicago	**1983** U.S. troops invade Grenada
1968 Richard Nixon elected president	**1984** Reagan reelected president
1969 First man on the moon	**1985** Mikhail Gorbachev becomes new Russian leader
1970 United States invades Cambodia	
1970 Kent State demonstrations	**1986** Space shuttle *Challenger* disaster
1971 Pentagon Papers case	**1986** Iran-Contra scandal
1971 Nixon visits China	**1987** Black Monday stock market crash
1972 Democratic Headquarters at the Watergate burglarized	**1988** George Bush elected president
	1988 Terrorist bomb on Pan Am Flight 103
1972 Nixon reelected	**1989** United States invades Panama
1973 *Roe v. Wade* makes abortion legal	**1989** Berlin Wall comes down
1974 Nixon resigns; Gerald Ford becomes new president	**1991** Communism ends in the Soviet Union
	1991 Gulf War
1975 Vietnam War ends	**1992** William Jefferson Clinton elected president
1976 Jimmy Carter elected president	
1978 *Bakke v. University of California* decided	**1993** World Trade Center bombed
	1993 Compound of religious extremists burns at Waco, Texas
1978 Camp David peace agreement between Israel and Egypt	**1994** Republicans gain control of House
1979 American hostages taken by Iran	**1995** U.S. troops in Bosnia
1980 Ronald Reagan elected president	**1995** Oklahoma City bombing
1980 Iran releases American hostages	**1996** Clinton re-elected
1981 Reagan signs biggest tax cut in American history	**1996** Unabomber captured
	1998 Clinton scandals investigated
1982 United States sends troops to Lebanon	**1999** Clinton impeached but not convicted

Look at the Mind Map and summarize which of the themes are still important in America at the end of the twentieth century.

As you look at each of the major themes—terrorism, presidents in crisis, foreign policy changes, and Supreme Court decisions—look at newspapers and watch television news shows, and you will be able to see how these themes play out in your life.

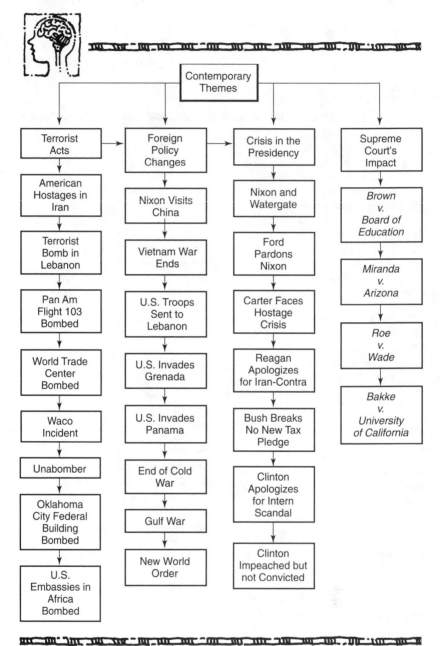

Contemporary Themes

Terrorist Acts
- American Hostages in Iran
- Terrorist Bomb in Lebanon
- Pan Am Flight 103 Bombed
- World Trade Center Bombed
- Waco Incident
- Unabomber
- Oklahoma City Federal Building Bombed
- U.S. Embassies in Africa Bombed

Foreign Policy Changes
- Nixon Visits China
- Vietnam War Ends
- U.S. Troops Sent to Lebanon
- U.S. Invades Grenada
- U.S. Invades Panama
- End of Cold War
- Gulf War
- New World Order

Crisis in the Presidency
- Nixon and Watergate
- Ford Pardons Nixon
- Carter Faces Hostage Crisis
- Reagan Apologizes for Iran-Contra
- Bush Breaks No New Tax Pledge
- Clinton Apologizes for Intern Scandal
- Clinton Impeached but not Convicted

Supreme Court's Impact
- *Brown v. Board of Education*
- *Miranda v. Arizona*
- *Roe v. Wade*
- *Bakke v. University of California*

CHAPTER FLASHBACK:

We ended Chapter Ten at an important point. Lyndon Johnson decided not to seek reelection in 1968 after demonstrations against the war in Vietnam reached a peak and after he had a poor showing in the New Hampshire presidential primary. These incidents ushered in a series of remarkable events that made 1968 a year to remember.

1968—A YEAR OF TURMOIL

Soon after Johnson announced that he was not seeking reelection, Robert F. Kennedy, brother of the former president, entered the race for president. He had the Kennedy charisma, and he ran urging an end to the war in Vietnam and promising to address the issues of discrimination and poverty in America. In the middle of his campaign, the tragic assassination of Martin Luther King, Jr., followed by race riots in many of the country's cities, brought to light the widening gap between white and black America.

SHERLOCK EYEWITNESS ACCOUNT:

Look at the following excerpt from a speech King gave the day before he was killed:

Well, I don't know what will happen now. We've got some difficult days ahead. But it doesn't matter with me now. Because I've been to the mountain top. And I don't mind. Like anybody, I would like to live a long life. Longevity has its place. But I'm not concerned about that now. I just want to do God's will. And He's allowed me to go up to the mountain. And I've looked over. And I've seen the promised land. I may not get there with you. But I want you to know tonight, that we, as a people will get to the promised land. And I'm happy, tonight. I'm not

worried about anything. I'm not fearing any man. Mine
eyes have seen the glory of the coming of the Lord.

Why do you think many of King's supporters believed he was
a prophet? How do you evaluate the importance of King's
contributions?

As we discussed in the last chapter, King was considered
a catalyst for the civil rights movement. Like Gandhi in India,
he believed in nonviolent protest as the means of achieving
his goal. The last speech he gave almost predicted his
untimely death, "I've seen the promised land." Little did
anyone realize that the next day he would start that journey.

 HISTORICAL TIDBIT:

In August 1998, the attorney general of the
United States ordered a review of the
circumstances surrounding the King assassination. The
purpose of the review was to determine if there was a
conspiracy.

Robert F. Kennedy attended King's funeral and urged
the country not to pursue a violent course. After winning the
California primary, violence took the life of the New York
senator when Jordanian Sirhan Sirhan shot him in June
1968. The country mourned another Kennedy.

 HISTORICAL TIDBIT:

Robert F. Kennedy's assassin, Sirhan
Sirhan, was sentenced to life imprisonment
for the crime he committed.

The year's violent events continued as the Democrats met
in Chicago to nominate their candidate for president. At this
convention, rioting took place and the leaders of the riots
who were arrested became known as the "Chicago Seven."

The Chicago Seven were all involved in the antiwar movement. Some were more radical than others, but they all were leaders and were arrested for stirring up the demonstrators. They were put on trial, but even though there were convictions, there were no long jail terms.

THE ELECTION AND PRESIDENCY OF RICHARD NIXON

The year concluded with the election of Richard Nixon as president of the United States. Let's take a look at his presidency and career, which spanned three decades.

President Richard Milhous Nixon was perhaps the most complicated politician the modern-day office of the presidency has seen. On the one hand, he had a real sense of what he felt the **silent majority** wanted.

Silent majority—Nixon's phrase used to describe what he believed to be the majority of Americans who supported his policies.

On the other hand, his distrust of the media and his abuse of power ultimately brought down his presidency.

The high points

Without a doubt, Nixon's foreign policy after the Vietnam War ended created his legacy. They included:

- **Disarmament talks with the Soviet Union**, called the Strategic Arms Limitations Talks (SALT). These talks resulted in an important breakthrough in the nuclear arms race. The result was that limits were placed on long-range nuclear missiles and defensive missiles.
- Perhaps his greatest foreign policy achievement was **the normalization of relations with China**. His historic visit in 1972 resulted in the establishment of diplomatic relations with the Communist Chinese.
- The **Nixon Doctrine** was established.

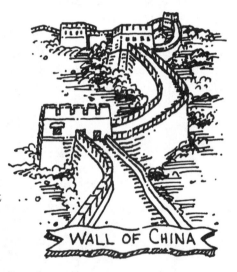

WALL OF CHINA

Nixon Doctrine—Nations of Asia would have to defend themselves and could not rely on the United States for massive aid.

- In the **conflict in the Middle East**, the United States and Nixon's secretary of state Henry Kissinger were solidly behind Israel.

The low points

- Trying to end the war in Vietnam. Running on a platform in 1968 to end the war in Vietnam in an honorable way, Nixon's answer was called **Vietnamization**, the return of American troops while maintaining and supporting the South Vietnamese.
  Unfortunately for Nixon, the slow progress and his secret escalation of the war in Cambodia laid the groundwork for the biggest political scandal in American History—Watergate.
- **Events like Kent State.** Students demonstrated after they learned about Nixon giving the green light to bomb Cambodia.

The Kent State incident brought to light how the antiwar movement had an impact on our foreign policy. Nixon, though critical of the students, felt more and more pressure to end the war. As a result, he began to take actions that in the end seriously hurt his presidency.

- **The Supreme Court decision in the Pentagon Papers case.** After massive demonstrations in Washington, D.C., classified papers related to the U.S. involvement in Vietnam were released to *The New York Times* by the author, Daniel Ellsberg. After the initial publication of a portion of these papers, Nixon obtained an order to have *The New York Times* stop the publication on the grounds of national security. The Supreme Court, in the case *New York Times v. United States,* ruled that the paper had the right under the First Amendment to print the story.

Watergate

Nixon gave the go-ahead to a secret group called the "plumbers" to initiate secret illegal actions such as breaking into the psychiatrist's office where the files of Daniel Ellsberg (the person responsible for handing the Pentagon papers over to *The New York Times*) were kept. Plans were approved to break into the Brookings Institute, a Washington-based policy organization, and to coordinate **dirty tricks**.

Dirty tricks—Secret efforts made by Nixon's campaign to disrupt the Democrats during the 1972 campaign.

The president's closest advisors, John Ehrlichman and Bob Haldeman, as well as the former Attorney General, John Mitchell, also took part in the cover-up. *The Washington Post* and its investigative journalists, Bob Woodward and Carl Bernstein, with the aid of a secret source called "Deep Throat" helped uncover the scandal.

An outgrowth of this group was formed in June 1972 when plans were approved to break into the Watergate offices of the head of the Democratic party. The burglars were caught and the Watergate scandal began. For over two years the nation watched a president stonewall an investigation. Then, when it was discovered that Nixon had a voice-actuated taping system in the White House, the investigation shifted. A special prosecutor, Archibald Cox, was fired in what became known as the "Saturday Night Massacre." The Supreme Court decided unanimously, in a case called the *United States v. Nixon,* that no man is above the law, ordering Nixon to release the tapes. The "smoking gun" tape was released, proving that Nixon participated in the cover-up of the investigation of the Watergate break-in, and Nixon was forced to resign.

Because of the Watergate scandal, for the first time, a sitting president had to resign from office.

The Watergate scandal is the "mother" of all political scandals. The event reads like a detective story. After his resignation and his pardon from his successor, Gerald Ford, Nixon began to enjoy a reputation as an elder statesman. He wrote several books, and expressed some sorrow over Watergate.

HISTORICAL TIDBIT:

The burglars responsible for the Watergate break-in were caught on a routine inspection by a security officer working in the Watergate office complex.

THE ROLE OF THE SUPREME COURT

As we alluded to in describing Nixon's downfall, the Supreme Court played a very important role. Besides deciding on Nixon's actions related to Watergate, the Court's influence steadily grew from the time it decided that segregation was illegal in 1954. Let's look at some cases that illustrate that point.

Miranda v. Arizona (1966)

Established that police had to inform accused criminals at the time they were arrested of their right to remain silent and their right to ask for an attorney.

Roe v. Wade (1972)

The Court decided that abortion is a constitutional right and declared that states could not make it illegal.

Bakke v. University of California (1978)

The Court ruled that a white medical student had to be admitted to a medical school, making the school's quota system illegal. But the court also said that race could be used as a factor in college admissions. This is called *affirmative action*.

Find out more about the Supreme Court, its history, and its cases and listen to audio from the oral arguments at the Northwestern University Supreme Court site at:

http://oyez.org

The Supreme Court's rulings in these cases were very significant. Like the Brown case, they established what is called precedent, setting a legal standard for these issues. In fact, these three areas are still very much in the news today.

PRESIDENTIAL CRISES

The final part of this chapter will follow the highlights of the presidencies of Gerald Ford, Jimmy Carter, Ronald Reagan, George Bush, and Bill Clinton. Each of these presidents faced serious domestic and foreign policy crises. The way they handled them determined how successful they were as president.

Gerald Ford

Gerald Ford had the difficult job of trying to heal the country's wounds after the Watergate scandal led to Richard Nixon's resignation, and after the conclusion of the controversial war in Vietnam. Ford's crisis resulted in:

- The pardoning of Richard Nixon. This action prevented any further prosecution of the former president of crimes related to Watergate. It was a key factor in why Ford lost his bid for reelection.
- Trying to deal with the high inflation and poor economy. The state of the economy was very poor during Ford's administration.
- Giving amnesty to antiwar activists who fled to Canada to avoid the military draft. During the war in Vietnam, many individuals who were against the war moved to Canada to avoid being drafted. Ford gave amnesty to those who were convicted, which ended any legal penalty they received. Even though Nixon successfully negotitated a peace treaty with North Vietnam, which, in effect, turned over the fighting of the war to South Vietnam, the war did not officially end until 1975. North Vietnamese troops took over the capital of South Vietnam and the country became united under a Communist government. One of the consequences of this long and difficult war was the passage of the **War Powers Act** by Congress in 1973.

War Powers Act—This 1973 act created restrictions on the part of a president who wanted to send troops into battle for a defined period without a declaration of war.

Bitterness lasted for years in this country. Vietnam veterans were angered that they did not get recognition for fighting the war. For many, the homecoming was a sad one. The veterans asked the government to build a memorial honoring the over 50,000 who were killed in the war. It was commissioned in 1980, and the wall listing the dead was built in 1982.

The visitors to the wall include people who want to honor those who served, as well as relatives and friends of the soldiers who died. Many leave flowers and other mementos at the base of the wall. They are collected each day and some have been placed on a permanent display at the Smithsonian Institution's Museum of American History. What kind of memorabilia would you leave if you had known a soldier who died in Vietnam?

Jimmy Carter—the peanut farmer from Georgia

In the election of 1976, an unknown governor from Georgia, Jimmy Carter, got the Democratic nomination for president. In a very close election, he defeated Gerald Ford. The peanut farmer from Georgia pledged to return morality to government, but unfortunately for him he was faced by both domestic and foreign policy crises that crippled his administration.

Throughout his term, the country was facing economic

hardship in the form of high inflation and high unemployment. The Arab oil nations made it difficult to get oil, and large lines at gas pumps were the order of the day.

On the positive side, Carter was able to negotiate an historic peace between Israel and Egypt, called the *Camp David Accords*. But the public lost faith in President Carter after Iran captured over fifty Americans from the American Embassy in Iran and held them hostage for over a year.

Sometimes former presidents achieve more respect after they leave office. This is true of Jimmy Carter. After leaving office, he and his wife Rosalynn dedicated themselves to fighting disease, hunger, poverty, and oppression. They are very involved in the building project, Habitat for Humanity. They personally have gone to Third World countries, and have supervised elections in countries whose citizens were involved in civil wars.

Ronald Reagan—the Great Communicator

Hollywood actor turned politician, Ronald Reagan easily defeated Jimmy Carter in 1980 to become, at age 70, the oldest elected president of the United States. At his inauguration, the country waited for Iran to release the American hostages and, immediately following his oath of office, word came that they were released. Reagan's two administrations were characterized by his ability to communicate with the American people, his desire to shrink the size of government, the tough stand he took toward communism, which led to the eventual downfall of the Soviet Union, and problems the country faced with terrorism and tragedy. Let's look at some of the key events:

- Domestically, Reagan addressed the issues of high unemployment and high inflation. He signed into law the largest tax cut in American history. The economy began to turn around. Along with these reforms, he also favored the downsizing of the government, but he insisted on maintaining a strong defense. As a result, though the country was generally on an upward economic swing, the budget deficit—the fact that more money was spent than taken in—increased dramatically. In 1987 the stock market had its largest percentage one-day loss in its recorded history.

- The country's problems in the Middle East continued during the Reagan years. Marines had to be sent to Lebanon in 1982 to help keep the peace. In 1983 terrorists bombed the U.S. Marine barracks there, killing more than 200 soldiers.

- Reagan had a sense of the dramatic. Shortly after the marines were murdered in Lebanon, Reagan saw a threat to American medical students who were studying at the school on the Caribbean island of Grenada. He ordered American troops to invade the country to protect the students. Many newspaper editorials were critical of the action and some called it a way of diverting attention from the terrorist attack in Lebanon.

- After Reagan's reelection to a second term, and with a new Soviet leader, Mikhail Gorbachev, negotiations began to reduce tensions between the two superpowers. The results came after a number of summit meetings that looked more like a poker game. Reagan played hardball and refused to back down on the development of a new defense system called the *Strategic Defense Initiative*. The Soviet Union finally agreed to reduce nuclear armaments in what became known as the *Strategic Arms Limitation Talks (SALT)*. It became apparent that Gorbachev represented a new kind of leader. He urged free discussion of domestic reform, which he called *glasnost*, and he developed a restructuring of the economic policy called *perestroika*. What Gorbachev failed to realize was that these reforms would open up a much larger reform movement that spread to the Communist countries in Eastern Europe and eventually led to the downfall of communism in the Soviet Union.

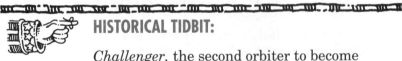

HISTORICAL TIDBIT:

The Strategic Defense Initiative was called "Star Wars" because it involved a series of satellites circling Earth having the capability of intercepting enemy missiles fired from Earth. The defense system was never built because it was too expensive.

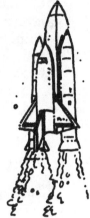

- Reagan's strength as a man who was in touch with the American public contributed to his being called the Great Communicator. His speaking abilities became evident during the campaign for re-election when one of the positive themes was "morning in America." He survived an assassination attempt during his first administration and joked about it while he was waiting for surgery.
- Reagan's talent as a communicator to the people was tested in one of our worst disasters. In January 1986, the space shuttle *Challenger* was scheduled to lift off with a civilian teacher on board. After what looked like a flawless take-off, the spaceship exploded, killing the entire crew. Reagan, in an emotional speech to the survivors and the nation, helped begin the healing process.

HISTORICAL TIDBIT:

Challenger, the second orbiter to become operational at Kennedy Space Center, was named after an American Naval research vessel that sailed the Atlantic and Pacific oceans during the 1870s. The *Apollo 17* lunar module also carried the name of "Challenger." *Challenger* joined NASA fleet of reusable winged spaceships in July 1982. It flew nine successful space shuttle missions. On January 28, 1986, the *Challenger* and its seven-member crew were lost 73 seconds after launch when a booster failure resulted in the breakup of the vehicle.

The *Challenger* disaster, like the assassination of John F. Kennedy, was an event that remains etched in memory. People never forget where they were when they heard about it. Is there an historical event in your lifetime that you will never forget?

- Reagan's popularity and job approval was high during much of his presidency; however, one event became the crisis for Ronald Reagan. It was called the Iran-Contra affair and it involved an illegal trading of arms by the United States to Iran in return for release of American hostages held in the Middle East. To make matters worse, the profits from the arms sales would then be used to illegally fund rebels fighting a Communist-supported government in Nicaragua. Reagan at first claimed these actions were legitimate, but after an independent review and congressional hearings, he had to admit he was responsible for the actions of others in his administration and admitted to the country he had made mistakes in not being aware of what was going on. Others involved in the affair were convicted of obstruction of justice and perjury. When George H. W. Bush was elected president, he pardoned some of the people involved.

- Reagan's two terms as president ended with the public generally supporting his policies. Though the country suffered a terrible economic setback in 1987, Reagan left office with one of the highest approval ratings of any second-term president.

HISTORICAL TIDBIT:

Ronald Reagan received more electoral votes than any candidate in presidential history when he was re-elected in 1984.

George H. W. Bush—Creating a New World Order

Ronald Reagan's vice president, George H. W. Bush, was the recipient of Reagan's popularity when he was elected president in 1988. Bush was a former congressman and former director of the Central Intelligence Agency. His presidency was marked by a struggle to keep the economy moving and a successful foreign policy highlighted by the end of the Cold War and the beginning of a new foreign policy era called the New World Order. Let's look at some of these events that illustrate how Bush faced crisis in his presidency.

The End of the Cold War

By 1989 most of Eastern Europe had been swept up in the reform movement and established new democratic governments. In 1991 an attempted overthrow of the Soviet government failed when Boris Yeltsin successfully took control. Events moved rapidly and the net result was the end of the Soviet Union and the birth of the Russian Federation, made up of independent republics.

The Gulf War

Bush's greatest crisis came in the form of an attempt by Iraqi leader Saddam Hussein to take over Kuwait and threaten the rest of the Middle East. Bush, along with the United Nations, set a date and threatened to bomb Iraq if they did not withdraw their troops by that date. In January 1991, the Gulf War began with a coalition of countries led by the United States. After a month of relentless bombing, the United States led an invasion against Iraq, and after 100 hours successfully regained control of Kuwait. Bush's popularity at home was, according to polls, over 90 percent approval. After the war ended, Bush stated that a new era in foreign policy had begun. He called it the New World Order and it was characterized by the United States leading peacekeeping operations with the assistance of the United Nations and the North Atlantic Treaty Organization (NATO).

William Jefferson Clinton— the "Comeback Kid"

The election of 1992 brought a relative unknown to the political scene. Bill Clinton was governor of Arkansas for two terms and had earned the reputation as a moderate Democrat. His history as a politician was a mix of accomplishments and personal failures. In 1998, Clinton became only the second president to be impeached by the House of Representatives. He was charged with *perjury* (lying under oath) and *obstruction of justice* (taking action to prevent judicial proceedings to go forward). Clinton was found not guilty by the Senate and he remained in office. Though his presidency had been threatened, he survived as he had many times before in his political career and lived up to his nickname, the "comeback kid."

The Election of 1992

Clinton had the advantage of challenging the incumbent, George H. W. Bush, by attacking Bush's broken promise of "Read my lips, no new taxes." As popular as Bush was when he led the nation in the Gulf War, the country was facing an economic recession in 1992. Bill Clinton and a new third party candidate, Texas billionaire Ross Perot, both attacked Bush's economic policies. Though Clinton was criticized for character flaws, he waged a focused campaign and beat Bush.

Look at the results from the election:

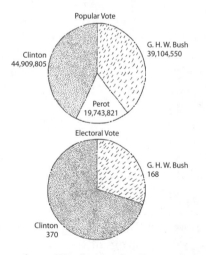

Popular Vote

Clinton 44,909,805

G. H. W. Bush 39,104,550

Perot 19,743,821

Electoral Vote

G. H. W. Bush 168

Clinton 370

Sherlock's Question: Explain why Perot did not get any electoral votes even though he received almost 20 million votes.

The presidential inauguration is a political tradition that establishes the start of a new president's term of office. It has pomp and circumstance—a formal speech and inaugural balls. Millions of people participate in the event either by attending it live or watching it on television. Many times, presidents have clearly defined the themes of their administration. Clinton's first inauguration attempted to establish a new direction for America.

The Clinton Era

Clinton's two terms as president have been marked by an economy that has been the strongest in the nation's history, but Clinton has also lived up to his name as the "comeback kid." After the Democrats lost control of Congress, Clinton was able to get reelected in 1996. His job approval during most of his presidency, especially during his second term, was well over 50 percent. He had the capacity to "feel the pain" of the American people as they faced the tragedies of terrorism when the World Trade Center was bombed by Arab terrorists in 1993 and the Federal Building in Oklahoma City was destroyed in 1995; 168 were killed.

President Clinton was quick to respond to these incidents. He went on national television to assure the American public that the country would not stand for violence. He attended the Oklahoma City memorial and made one of the most moving and dramatic speeches of his career.

Bill Clinton continued to face crises in his presidency. He continued the foreign policy started by George H. W. Bush by sending American troops to Haiti in 1992, to Somalia in 1993, and to Bosnia in 1995.

The Clinton administration also had to deal with the threat of domestic terrorism from individuals who called themselves militiamen. Timothy McVeigh, convicted of the Oklahoma City Federal Building bombing, was an example of a person who called himself a militiaman. He believed that the federal government threatened the personal freedom of individuals. He planned the bombing on the anniversary of another event, the destruction of the compound of religious extremists by the FBI at Waco, Texas, in 1993.

The rise of violence in the United States by both foreign forces and people who are unhappy with the government is a disturbing trend. Events such as Waco and the Unabomber sending mail bombs to people connected with the advancement of computer technology raise very important questions and concerns.

Scandals

The final chapter of Clinton's presidency involved a series of scandals connected to his administration and to himself personally. They have all been given a scandal name and represent the negative side of his presidency. Let's look at them briefly.

Whitewater—A failed land deal in Arkansas when Clinton was governor in which Clinton and his wife, Hillary Rodham Clinton, were accused of illegal dealings. The controversy continued while he was president.

Travelgate—Misuse of the White House travel office by the president and his wife after the people working there were fired.

Filegate—Accessing by Clinton's aides of hundreds of FBI files of individuals, some of whom were political opponents.

Campaign finance abuses—Both Clinton and his vice president, Al Gore, as well as the Democratic party were accused of raising campaign money from illegal sources.

Interngate—Questions related to perjury, obstruction of justice, and abuse of power related to the personal relationship of the president with a White House intern.

These scandals led to investigations by Independent Counsel Kenneth Starr, who had the responsibility for investigating the charges and sending a report to Congress if he found evidence of impeachable offenses. In September 1998, Starr advised the House of Representatives that President Clinton had committed possible "high crimes and misdemeanors," the language of the Constitution that could result in his impeachment. In December 1998, the House of Representatives voted to impeach President Clinton, charging him with perjury and obstruction of justice. The vote was highly controversial and criticized by over two-thirds of the American people because almost all the Republicans voted for impeachment, while almost all the Democrats voted against it.

When the trial began in the Senate in January 1999, President Clinton became the first elected president and only the second president since Andrew Johnson to face removal from office. The trial lasted 21 days. Testimony from the White House intern who the president had a sexual relationship with as well as the report submitted by the special prosecutor did not convince the Senators to convict Clinton. Neither charge received the two-thirds majority needed to remove the president from office.

The legacy of Bill Clinton's presidency remains highly debatable. Historians will certainly evaluate the two terms of William Jefferson Clinton. Whatever happens, if you have learned the many lessons contained in this book and followed these events, you should be able to reach your own conclusions about the impact of these scandals on the institution of the presidency.

SHERLOCK'S PRESIDENTIAL MADNESS:

Match the president with the event that occurred in his administration

Richard Nixon	Iran-Contra
Jimmy Carter	Desert Storm
Ronald Reagan	Impeachment
George H. W. Bush	Iran hostage crisis
Bill Clinton	Watergate

CHAPTER TWELVE

The New Millennium

WALL ST

BARACK OBAMA

GEORGE
W. BUSH
2001-2009

I can hear you, the rest of the world hears you. And the people who knocked these buildings down will hear all of us soon.

—President George W. Bush at Ground Zero
at the World Trade Center site September 14, 2001

Time Line (2000–2008)

2000 Former First Lady Hillary Clinton elected New York senator

2000 Presidential election contested; Supreme Court declared Bush the winner; Al Gore won popular vote

2001 President Bush signed largest tax-cut law in twenty years

2001 Terrorists attacked World Trade Center and Pentagon; More than 3,000 Americans killed; Islamic militant Osama Bin Laden behind attacks

2001 The Patriot Act, a law aimed at increasing the government's ability to discover terrorists, passes

2001 The United States invaded Afghanistan; Taliban regime defeated in two months

2002 President Bush describes Iraq, Iran, and North Korea as "axis of evil" in State of the Union speech

2002 In response to scandals at several major corporations, Bush signed corporate reform bill

2002 No Child Left Behind education reform act signed into law

2002 Republicans retake the Senate and increase majority in House in midterm elections

2002 Department of Homeland Security created

2003 Space Shuttle *Columbia* exploded on re-entry, killing the crew

2003 U.S. invaded Iraq in response to intelligence driven threats of weapons of mass destruction; "Mission accomplished" sign greets President Bush as he declares an end to first phase of the war

2003 California Governor Gray Davis "recalled" (California voters sign a petition that forces the governor to resign and a new election is held); Hollywood actor Arnold Schwarzenegger elected

2004 Massachusetts becomes the first state to allow gay marriages

2004 Bipartisan September 11 commission criticizes the government's handling of terrorist attacks

2004 Final government report found no weapons of mass destruction in Iraq

2004 Sectarian violence in Iraq increases and U.S. military casualties rise

2004 George W. Bush re-elected to second term, defeating Massachusetts Senator John Kerry; Republicans make gains in Congress

2004 President Ronald Reagan dies at the age of 93 after a long struggle with Alzheimer's disease

2005 First female Supreme Court Justice Sandra Day O'Connor resigns from Supreme Court; Chief Justice William Rehnquist dies; John Roberts named new Chief Justice and Samuel Alito new associate justice

2005 Hurricane Katrina devastated New Orleans; federal, state, and local governments criticized for slow response

2005 National Security Agency's secret spying activities revealed

2006 First veto used by President Bush on bill to allow expansion of stem cell research

2006 Democrats retake control of Congress; Nancy Pelosi elected first woman Speaker of the House

2007 Nation mourned death of President Gerald Ford

2007 Bush announced "troop surge" in Iraq; surge reduced violence and increased Iraq's security; more than 4,000 Americans have died in the war

2007 Law to increase minimum wage signed

2007 George W. Bush signed law to expand wiretapping of Americans suspected of possible terrorist activities

2007 Attorney General Gonzales resigned after investigation of firings of U.S. attorneys

2008 Historic presidential primaries began; Senator Barack Obama defeated Senator Hillary Clinton and became the first African-American to receive nomination; Senator John McCain won Republican nomination and chose Governor Sarah Palin, the first female Republican vice-presidential nominee

2008 Housing and economic crisis dominated election campaign

2008 Economic downturn resulted in record job losses and a recession

2008 Barack Obama elected 44th President of the United States

Looking at contemporary history is a challenge. Sherlock completes your interactive journey through time by discussing issues and themes that were in the news over the last eight years.

Look at the Mind Map and summarize which themes have dominated America in the new century.

As you look at the major themes—political and global—look at newspapers, browse the Internet, and watch the news on television, and you will be able to see how these themes play out in your life.

CHAPTER FLASHBACK:

We ended Chapter Eleven at an important transition. Bill Clinton survived impeachment and the end of his administration was right around the corner. The nation had gone through a decade of peace and prosperity and Clinton's vice-president, Al Gore, was the obvious choice to run for president.

2000—A NEW CENTURY AND NEW CHALLENGES

As the clock approached midnight on December 31, 1999, the world held its breath. Concerns that Y2K (the year 2000) would upset computers around the world spread like a virus. As the first time zone celebrated the new millennium, and computers worked, people breathed a sigh of relief. The new century began with an optimism that would soon be shattered by a disputed presidential election and terrorist attacks that would usher in a brand new type of warfare.

HISTORICAL TIDBIT:

As a result of the Y2K fears, the U.S. government responded to the threat by passing the Year 2000 Information and Readiness Disclosure Act, working with businesses to ensure readiness.

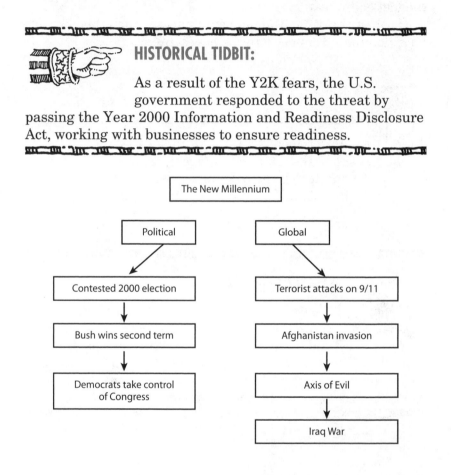

SHERLOCK CHALLENGE:

As you read about the political and global challenges of the twenty-first century make a list of things you would bury in a time capsule that would be dug up at the end of the first decade.

POLITICAL CHALLENGE AT THE BEGINNING OF THE 21ST CENTURY

The Election and Presidency of George W. Bush

The first campaign for the presidency in the new century resulted in an election that was in dispute for five weeks. The U.S. Supreme Court finally resolved it in a decision that indirectly gave victory to Texas Governor George W. Bush by stopping a vote recount in Florida. Governor Bush, the son of the forty-first President George H. W. Bush, defeated Vice President Al Gore. Third-party candidate Ralph Nader, running on the Green party ticket, took away enough Democratic votes from Gore to give Bush an electoral victory in Florida and other key states.

 **HISTORICAL TIDBIT**

The only other time a son of a former president was elected to the presidency was the sixth president John Quincy Adams in 1824. Also George W. Bush was only the fourth president in American history to lose the popular vote while winning the electoral vote.

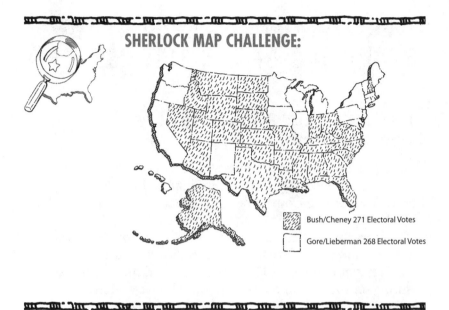

SHERLOCK MAP CHALLENGE:

Bush/Cheney 271 Electoral Votes

Gore/Lieberman 268 Electoral Votes

Look at the 2000 electoral map. Explain why Gore won more popular votes than Bush even though Bush won a majority of the electoral votes.

Looking at the map you will see that Gore won more states than Bush with large urban populations. Beating Bush in New York, Pennsylvania, Illinois, and California gave Gore more popular votes than Bush.

With the country divided over the election for president, the Republicans also remained in control of the Congress. Even though the Senate was equally divided, 50-50, the Republicans had a majority because Vice-President Dick Cheney as presiding officer of the Senate cast the tie-breaking vote. It was the first time since 1952 that the Republicans controlled both the executive and legislative branches of government. One of the unique aspects of this election was the voters in New York picking former First Lady Hillary Clinton to be their senator. This paved the way for Senator Clinton to run for president in 2008.

Divided government—When one branch of government is controlled by one party (for example, the presidency is controlled by a Republican) and one or two houses of Congress is controlled by the other party (for instance the House of Representatives and the Senate have a majority of Democrats.)

SHERLOCK BIOGRAPHY SPOTLIGHT: LAURA BUSH

Laura Bush was 54 years old when she became the nation's First Lady. She was formerly a librarian and schoolteacher and grew up in Midland, Texas. Her role model was the former First Lady, Barbara Bush. As First Lady, Laura Bush was an advocate for education, encouraging children to read. The experience she had as First Lady of Texas helped her in the transition to her role as First Lady of the United States.

The Election of 2004

George W. Bush ran for re-election in 2004 against Vietnam war hero Massachusetts Senator John Kerry. George W. Bush used **incumbency** and the argument that he was the best suited to wage a war against terrorism to his advantage and that it was a bad time to change presidents. The events of September 11 became the backdrop to the 2004 campaign. Bush emphasized his "steady leadership." He campaigned as a supporter of "family values" and smaller government. He successfully tied the Iraq war to terrorism, while characterizing his opponent as a "flip flopper." He won both the popular vote and the electoral vote, and the Republicans kept control of the Congress.

Incumbent—a person running for re-election to an electoral office. George W. Bush was the incumbent in 2004 because he was running for re-election.

SHERLOCK MAP CHALLENGE:

Bush 286 Electoral Votes

Kerry 252 Electoral Votes

Compare the 2000 electoral map to the 2004 electoral map.

In 2004 Bush won New Mexico and Iowa giving him an additional fifteen electoral votes and with increased voter turnout won a popular vote majority.

Key Domestic Events during Bush Presidency

Note: The events of 9/11 will be covered in the next section.

Sherlock Headlines of the Day

In looking at the domestic events during the Bush administration, Sherlock has created a series of newspaper headlines and short capsule summaries of the most important issues facing the United States. As you read these headlines, consider the impact these events have had on the lives of Americans.

- Bush legislative agenda includes largest tax cut in twenty years, No Child Left Behind education reform, corporate reform, Social Security reform, Medicare prescription drug benefit and comprehensive immigration reform

The four major legislative accomplishments passed during the Bush presidency were:

1. a tax cut that lowered the tax rates (2001)
2. the No Child Left Behind Act (2002), which created accountability standards for schools
3. a corporate reform bill that protected stockholders from corporate fraud
4. a prescription drug benefit for senior citizens (2003) that enabled them to acquire prescription drugs as part of Medicare

After Bush was re-elected in 2004, he proposed a major reform in the Social Security law that would have enabled some people to set up private accounts. His critics called this the "privatization of Social Security," and the reform never passed. Bush also proposed an immigration law that would have provided a way for the twelve million undocumented immigrants living in the United States to become citizens and increased border security. Because of opposition to citizenship for illegal aliens, the only part of the law to pass was the creation of a border fence and increased security measures.

- 2001—Space shuttle *Columbia* explodes killing all seven astronauts

In a scene that reminded Americans of the tragic explosion of the *Challenger* space shuttle in 1986, seven astronauts were killed when their space shuttle had a malfunction on re-entry because some insulation fell off the space shuttle during take-off.

SHERLOCK EYEWITNESS ACCOUNT:

It lasted over 30–45 seconds. It blew the doors open on various business in the area. We thought it was a couple of jet fighters that sometimes train over this area doing low fly-overs. A minute later we got reports coming in of debris coming down. No-one has been injured. Fortunately it happened at a time when not many people were up and about.

—Lieutenant Paul Peterson, of Nacogdoches Police, Dallas

Sherlock's **Question:** Knowing the risks, would you want to fly the space shuttle?

- 2003—California voters force Governor Davis to resign in what is called a "recall election," Hollywood actor Arnold Schwarzenegger elected new governor

California is one of a minority of states that allows voters to sign a petition that would force an elected official to resign from that office. In 2003 the voters were upset at the job California Governor Gray Davis was doing. Enough voters signed a petition that resulted in what is called a "recall." The recall vote, which dates back to the Progressive Era, was created to give voters a greater voice in their government.

- 2005—Sandra Day O'Connor resigns from the Supreme Court

The makeup of the Supreme Court changed dramatically during the Bush years. One of his campaign promises was to appoint "conservative" justices to the Supreme Court. He had his first opportunity when the first woman Supreme Court justice Sandra Day O'Connor, who was appointed in 1981 by Ronald Reagan, resigned from the court.

Key Quote from Sandra Day O'Connor

The courts of this country should not be the places where resolution of disputes begins. They should be the places where the disputes end after alternative methods of resolving disputes have been considered and tried.

Bush's appointment as O'Connor's replacement was federal judge John Roberts. When Chief Justice William Rehnquist, who served on the court for thirty-three years died, Bush elevated Roberts to Chief Justice. He then appointed federal court judge Samuel Alito to fill the O'Connor vacancy. Both choices were confirmed by the United States Senate.

Sherlock's **Question:** If you were a United States senator, what questions would you ask a nominee to the Supreme Court? How would you decide whether to vote for or against a person nominated to the court?

- Hurricane Katrina devastates Gulf coast; More than 1,800 die and millions are left homeless: New Orleans in ruins; Federal government criticized for slow response

In 2005, Hurricane Katrina hit the Gulf coast during one of the most active hurricane seasons. As a Category 4 storm, it caused major devastation along the Gulf Coast. New Orleans became the symbol of the devastation as a result of the failure of their levee system. Though all levels of government were criticized for a slow response, there was outrage against the federal government for its slow response. The agency responsible for emergency preparedness, FEMA (Federal Emergency Management Agency), took the brunt of the criticism. And when President Bush complimented the agency's head, Michael Brown stating, "You're doing a heck of a job Brownie," the news media and the American public became angrier.

KATRINA FACTS:

- Hurricane Katrina was one of the deadliest hurricanes in the history of the United States, killing over 1,800 people.

- Katrina was the largest hurricane of its strength to approach the United States in recorded history; its sheer size caused devastation over 100 miles (160 kilometers) from the storm's center.
- New Orleans' levee failures were found to be primarily the result of system design flaws, combined with the lack of adequate maintenance.
- Hurricane Katrina was the costliest hurricane in U.S. history, with $75 billion in estimated damages.

SHERLOCK EYEWITNESS ACCOUNT: INSIDE THE NEW ORLEANS SUPERDOME:

There are now 20,000 people inside the Superdome. The only medical personnel at the Superdome are Acadian Ambulance paramedics and EMT's and a small team of doctors and nurses from New Mexico. They are exhausted, understaffed and out of medical supplies. The only current source of medical supplies are those that Acadian is able to ferry in. Dialysis equipment is no longer functioning. Sick people are getting sicker. 30 people have now died in the Superdome, including one suicide.

There is no running water and sewage is overflowing in the bathrooms. There is no electricity or air conditioning (it is expected to be 95 degrees outside today). The back-up generators are expected to fail later this morning.

There is no plan to provide for an evacuation of the 30,000 people in the Superdome. There is no plan to evacuate the people trapped in their hotels and houses (who are almost or completely out of food and water)—when the floodwaters were still low enough, these people were simply told to "go to the Superdome." Now they are sitting outside the Superdome because there is no room inside.

Sherlock's Question: Who was the blame for the lack of response after Hurricane Katrina made landfall?

- Democrats regain control of Congress in the 2006 **midterm election**; Nancy Pelosi elected first woman Speaker of the House

Midterm election—Voters electing members of the United States Congress in the second year of a presidential administration. For example, 2006 was the midpoint of the second administration of George W. Bush.

As a result of voter unhappiness related to the war in Iraq and criticism of corruption by Republicans, the Democrats in 2006 regained control of both houses of Congress for the first time since 1994. They elected Nancy Pelosi as the first woman Speaker of the House. As the presiding officer of the House of Representatives, the Speaker of the House is second in line to become president if the president dies in office.

Sherlock's Question: How is the Speaker of the House elected?

Candidates for Speaker are nominated from the House floor by the members of their parties. Traditionally, one candidate from the majority party and one candidate from the minority party are nominated. The candidate who has the most votes becomes the Speaker, and since the Democrats held a majority of seats after the 2006 election, Nancy Pelosi was elected to that post.

- the United States faces an economic crisis

In the fall of 2008, the United States experienced its worse economic crisis since The Great Depression. There were bank failures, foreclosures on houses, unemployment reached a seven year high, and the greatest one day point loss in the stock market. The causes of this economic downturn were a housing market that collapsed and loans that banks made that could not be paid back. Congress responded by passing the Economic Stabilization Act, a $700 billion dollar rescue plan that many people described as a bailout for Wall Street and the banking industry.

Sherlock examines a new law: The Economic Stabilization Act provides:

- up to $700 billion loaned to banks who made poor credit loans that would have to be paid back to the taxpayers

- assistance to homeowners who have been caught up in the current mortgage crisis and are trying to save their homes
- limits on what is considered excessive salaries and bonuses, also called "golden parachutes," for executives of failed corporations
- an increase in the amount of money insured by the Federal Deposit Insurance Corporation from $100,000 to $250,000

Sherlock's **Question:** Compare the causes and solutions of the Great Depression to the 2008 economic crisis.

Historic 2008 Presidential Election

After a difficult and long primary battle, Republican nominee and Vietnam war hero John McCain faced off against the first-term Senator from Illinois, Barack Obama, the first African-American to receive a major party's nomination. Obama chose Delaware Senator Joseph Biden as his running mate. McCain selected first-term governor from Alaska Sarah Palin. During the primaries, Obama defeated Senator Hillary Clinton who as the former First Lady was looking to make history as the first elected woman president. Even though she lost, Mrs. Clinton had 18 million votes during the primary. One of the first appointments that the newly elected President Obama made was to select Hillary Clinton as Secretary of State. Senator McCain, whose campaign initially stalled, beat a field of ten Republican opponents. His choice of Palin represented only the second time in American history that a woman was selected as a major party running mate and was the first time the Republican party chose a woman.

It was a hard fought campaign with clear differences between Obama and McCain. The themes established by the candidates were "hope and change" for Obama and "experience and country first" for McCain. Ultimately a serious economic collapse, historically low job approval ratings for the Republican incumbent president George W. Bush, and an energized voter base resulted in a dramatic victory for Senator Obama. Winning 365 electoral votes and a 52–46 popular vote margin, Obama was the first

African-American elected president. Democrats also increased their majorities in the Senate and House of Representatives giving the newly elected president a mandate to achieve his goals.

SHERLOCK MAP CHALLENGE:

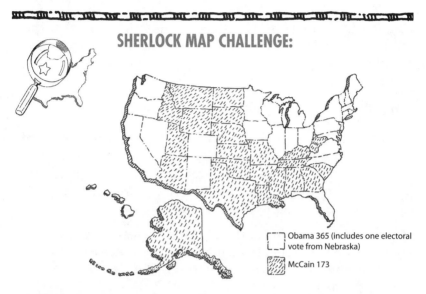

⬚ Obama 365 (includes one electoral vote from Nebraska)

▨ McCain 173

Compare the 2008 map with the electoral maps of 2000 and 2004.

BARACK OBAMA OFFICIAL UNITED STATES SENATOR BIOGRAPHY

Senator from Illinois; born in Honolulu, Hawaii, August 4, 1961; obtained early education in Jakarta, Indonesia, and Hawaii; continued education at Occidental College, Los Angeles, Calif.; received a B.A. in 1983 from Columbia University, New York City; worked as a community organizer in Chicago, Ill.; studied law at Harvard University, where he became the first African-American president of the Harvard Law Review, the famous legal journal, and

*received J.D. in 1991; lecturer on constitutional law,
University of Chicago; member, Illinois State Senate
1997–2004; elected as a Democrat to the U.S. Senate in
2004 for term beginning January 3, 2005.*

Sherlock's Question: What are the qualifications that the
United States Constitution establishes for President of the
United States?

The First Hundred Days

After President Obama's first hundred days were completed,
historians began the debate on how his agenda compares to
other presidents. There were a number of historic pieces of
legislation passed by Congress and signed into law by the
new president including:

- An extension of the Children's Health Insurance
  Policy that extended health insurance coverage for
  children, previously vetoed by former President
  Bush
- The Lily Ledbetter Act protecting women from
  pay discrimination in the workplace, a response
  to a Supreme Court ruling that prevented Ms.
  Ledbetter from suing after she discovered that she
  was earning less than her male cournterparts
- An Economic Recovery Act totaling close to
  $1 trillion that includes tax cuts for most
  Americans and job stimulus provisions. Related to
  this, the Obama administration also announced
  how the government will deal with the ailing bank
  industry, auto industry, and housing market

Whether historians conclude that Obama's legislation is
comparable to FDR's New Deal remains to be seen. President
Obama's job approval rating during his first hundred days
was among the highest of any new president. Coincidentally,
the cable network C-SPAN asked seventy-five historians
to rank the nation's presidents in various categories. Final
scores were tallied and the following list represented their
view of the top ten best and worse presidents:

The **Top Ten Presidents** are:

1. Lincoln
2. Washington
3. F.D. Roosevelt
4. Theodore Roosevelt
5. Truman
6. Kennedy
7. Jefferson
8. Eisenhower
9. Wilson
10. Reagan

The Worst Ten Presidents are:

33. Hayes
34. Hoover
35. Tyler
36. George W. Bush
37. Fillmore
38. Harding
39. W.H. Harrison
40. Pierce
41. A. Johnson
42. Buchanan

Sherlock's Question: What are the things historians look at when deciding the top ten and worse ten presidents?

GLOBAL CHALLENGES AT THE BEGINNING OF THE 21ST CENTURY

The War on Terror

We will direct every resource at our command, every means of diplomacy, every tool of intelligence, every instrument of law enforcement, every financial influence and every necessary weapon of war to the disruption and to the defeat of the global terror network. . . . Freedom and

fear are at war. . . . We will not tire, we will not falter, and we will not fail.
—President George W. Bush speaking to a joint session of Congress in 2001

In what President George W. Bush called "the first war of the 21st century," Islamic terrorists led by Osama Bin Laden, attacked the United States on September 11, 2001. Nearly 3,000 people from 80 nations were killed when two hijacked planes crashed into the World Trade Center Twin Towers in New York City. Among the dead were more than 300 New York City firemen and policemen responding to the scene after the two jets hit the buildings.

Just outside Washington, D.C., another hijacked plane crashed into the Pentagon, killing 180 military and civilian personnel along with everyone aboard the plane. A fourth hijacked plane crashed into a wooded area of southern Pennsylvania after the passengers on the plane attacked the hijackers. This plane was reportedly on its way to the White House or the Capitol.

SHERLOCK ROLE-PLAYING CHALLENGE:

Take the role of the President of the United States and decide what actions you would take in light of the terrorist attacks on the United States.

You should take into consideration the shock the country experienced as a result of this attack. Your decision should include what President George W. Bush ultimately outlined before a joint session of Congress in the aftermath of September 11:

1. Identify and pursue the terrorists responsible for the attacks. Form a coalition of countries that will join and support the United States. Inform Afghanistan's ruling Taliban government that they must turn over the Al Qaeda organization including Osama Bin Laden and warn other countries harboring terrorists that they would be held accountable.

2. Create a new cabinet position, the Office of Homeland Security.
3. Use federal government resources to help the massive cleanup in New York City.
4. Freeze the monetary assets of recognized terrorists.
5. Provide humanitarian aid to the people of Afghanistan and to refugees who fled that country.

In response to the terrorism attacks, Congress passed what it called The United States Patriot Act. The act's purpose was to expand the government's role in dealing with domestic terrorism.

SHERLOCK ANALYSIS:

Analyze the following provisions of the Patriot Act in light of many critics who believe the act restricts the civil liberties of Americans. The act:

- Gives the government the right to conduct secret searches and phone and Internet surveillance.
- Gives the government access to private records if there is evidence of possible terrorist activity.
- Permits the imprisonment of noncitizens without due process if there is evidence they are involved in terrorist plots

In addition to this act, the White House directed the National Security Agency to conduct secret wiretapping on the phone calls of Americans who were suspected to be in contact with terrorists in other countries. Newspapers uncovered this warrantless wiretapping, and a debate took place in the Congress whether it violated the Constitution. Ultimately, Congress passed a law that created guidelines.

The United States and Great Britain began a military attack against the military and terrorist targets in Afghanistan in October 2001. By the end of 2001, the Taliban had been defeated, and a new government was established in Afghanistan. Even though this action was hailed as a victory, by the summer of 2008, there was a resurgence of the Taliban in Afghanistan. As a result, more United States troops were assigned to fight in Afghanistan.

The Axis of Evil

During the State of the Union address in 2002, President George W. Bush said that there was an "axis of evil" that included North Korea, Iran, and Iraq. The United States pursued a policy that attempted to neutralize those countries' terrorist policies. The president made the point that all three countries were sponsors of state-supported terrorism and that they had the capability of using weapons of mass destruction including nuclear weapons and chemical warfare.

SHERLOCK MAP CHALLENGE:

Locate the countries on the map that make up the so-called axis of evil.

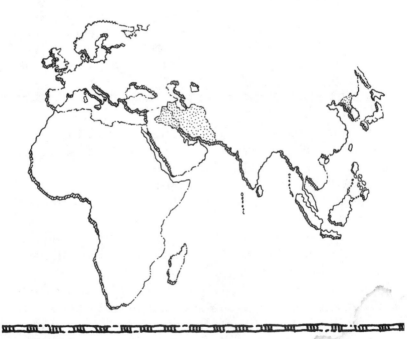

Operation Iraqi Freedom

In September 2003, President George W. Bush and Secretary of State Colin Powell addressed the United Nations and made the case that Iraq was a major terrorist threat. They accused Iraq of hiding weapons of mass destruction. The Bush administration received a vote from the congress giving the president whatever authority necessary to make Iraqi President Saddam Hussein comply with the United Nations resolutions directing him to turn over all weapons of mass destruction. Hussein claimed that there were no weapons and after UN inspectors failed to find any, the United States, citing national security, invaded Iraq in March 2003.

The United States-led invasion successfully crushed the government of Saddam Hussein and in a three-week period marched into Iraq's capital, Baghdad, where allied forces symbolically toppled a statue of the Iraqi leader. United States casualties were limited. On May 1, 2003, President Bush landed on an aircraft carrier and proclaimed the end of major combat in the war in front of a sign that read "Mission Accomplished."

However, between the spring of 2003 and 2006, peacekeeping efforts were met with stiff resistance. Saddam Hussein was captured, tried, and executed. Over 4,000 American soldiers were killed. Opposition to the war in the United States rose when it became evident that there were no weapons of mass destruction in Iraq. In June 2004, the United States turned over the country to a new government. More than 100,000 troops remained to support the new government. After Bush was re-elected in 2004, he pledged to keep American forces in Iraq until a stable government was formed and Iraqi troops could be trained to replace American soldiers. Elections were held, and a new parliament was established.

During 2005, violence among the Iraqi Sunni and Shiite factions increased. The country moved toward what was called a civil war after a Shiite mosque was destroyed. American casualties also increased. After the congressional midterm elections in 2006, President George W. Bush replaced the Secretary of Defense. Bush also ordered what he called a "troop surge" of an additional 30,000 troops to Iraq as "a new way forward" to end violence and provide security so that the government could stabilize. In the fall of 2008, the United States and Iraq reached an agreement that outlined a time frame for United States troop withdrawals if conditions on the ground continued to improve. President Obama established a more definite timeline in the early days of his administration.

SHERLOCK'S MATCHING MADNESS: THE NEW MILLENNIUM:

Match the following events with what happened during this new century.

Y2K	Name given after United States troops invaded Afghanistan
2000 Election	Name given after United States troops invaded Iraq
War on Terror	Name given by President George W. Bush to Iran, Iraq, and North Korea
The Patriot Act	What people referred to when the new century began
Operation Enduring Freedom	Additional troops sent to Iraq in 2006
Axis of Evil	Policy used to describe United States actions taken after the attacks on September 11
Operation Iraqi Freedom	Contested election resulting in George W. Bush winning first of two terms
2006 Midterm Election	Increased government wiretapping
The Surge	Election when Democrats took control of Congress

A FINAL NOTE

As you near the end of *Painless American History,* you should now see that American history is not so painful after all. Even though our journey through *Painless American History* is almost over, remember that the Internet can provide fascinating insights into our nation's past. The appendix that follows provides a comprehensive list of Internet sites for each chapter that will enhance your knowledge and understanding of American History. Though sites may change over time, if you use the title listed above each site and put it in an Internet search engine, the results of your search will provide similar places to explore.

APPENDIX— INTERNET RESOURCES

Chapter One

Avalon Project:
http://www.yale.edu/lawweb/avalon/chrono.htm

American History by Decades:
http://melvil.chicousd.org/decsg.html

Twentieth Century Documents/Vietnam War:
http://melvil.chicousd.org/decs6.html#Cold

Smithsonian American History Time Line:
http://www.si.edu/Encyclopedia_SI/nmah/timeline.htm

Library of Congress:
http://www.loc.gov

Library of Congress History Detective:
http://memory.loc.gov/learn/features/detect/detectiv.html

Enola Gay Controversy:
http://digital.lib.lehigh.edu/trial/enola/about/

Chapter Two

Anasazi Archaeology:
http://www.swcolo.org/tourism/archaeology/ahc.html

American History Sources for Students/Indigenous People:
http://www.sondra.net/links/k-native.htm

Biography of Leif Erickson by Kevin A. Weitemier:
http://www.mnc.net/norway/LeifErikson.htm

1492: An Ongoing Voyage:
http://sunsite.unc.edu/expo/1492.exhibit/Intro.html

Discovery's Web Biography of Verrazzano:
http://www.win.tue.nl/~engels/discovery/verrazzano.html

Discovery's Web: North America:
http://www.win.tue.nl/~engels/discovery/northam.html

Jamestown Settlement:
http://www.nationalcenter.org/SettlementofJamestown.html

The Association for the Preservation of Virginia Antiquities:
http://www.apva.org/history/index.html

Caleb Johnson's Mayflower Web Pages:
http://www.mayflowerhistory.com/

Essays on the United States of America and the Netherlands:
http://odur.let.rug.nl/~usa/E/newnetherlands/nlxx.htm

Chapter Three

The Original 13 Colonies:
http://www.timepage.org/spl/13colony.html

Visit New England:
http://www.visitnewengland.com/

The Thirteen Originals:
http://www.timepage.org/spl/13colony.html

Francis Bacon Web Site:
http://www.virginiaplaces.org/military/bacon.html

Create a blog:
http://www.blogger.com/home

The Library of Congress Exhibit: Religion and the Founding
of the American Republic:
http://lcweb.loc.gov/exhibits/religion/religion.html

The Salem Witch Trial:
http://www.law.umkc.edu/faculty/projects/ftrials/salem/
salem.htm

Salem Witch Museum:
http://www.salemwitchmuseum.com/

Poor Richards Almanck:
http://www.ushistory.org/FRANKLIN/quotable/singlehtml.htm

Franklin Institute's Portrait of Benjamin Franklin:
http://sln.fi.edu/franklin/rotten.html

Slave Narratives:
http://www.vgskole.net/prosjekt/slavrute/primary.htm

Chapter Four

Fort William Henry Museum:
http://www.lakegeorgehistorical.org/site_1.htm

Fort William Henry Massacre:
http://www.u-s-history.com/pages/h1175.html

French and Indian War:
http://www.frenchandindianwar250.org/

Boston Massacre Web Site:
http://www.law.umkc.edu/faculty/projects/ftrials/bostonmassacre/bostonmassacre.html

Boston Tea Party:
http://www.eyewitnesstohistory.com/teaparty.htm

Paul Revere's House:
http://www.paulreverehouse.org/

Freedom Trail Virtual Tour—page 69:
http://www.thefreedomtrail.org/

Colonial Hall's Founding Fathers' Site:
http://www.colonialhall.com/

National Archives Exhibit Room:
http://www.archives.gov/exhibits/charters/declaration.html

Chronological List of Battles and Actions:
http://www.revolutionary-war.info/timeline/

Differences between Colonial Forces and British Army:
http://www.pbs.org/ktca/liberty/perspectives_military.html

Loyalist Songs and Poetry of the Revolution:
http://www3.sympatico.ca/goweezer/theshack/songs.htm

Library of Congress—To Form a More Perfect Union:
http://memory.loc.gov/ammem/collections/continental/
intro01.html

Biographies of the Founding Fathers National Archives
Exhibit:
http://www.archives.gov/exhibits/charters/constitution_
founding_fathers.html

National Constitution Center:
http://www.constitutioncenter.org

White House for Kids:
http://www.whitehouse.gov/kids/

Government Agencies Home Page for Kids:
http://www.fedstats.gov/kids/index.html

Chapter Five

The George Washington Photo Album Collection:
http://www.pocanticohills.org/washington/images.htm

Washington's Home at Mount Vernon:
http://www.mountvernon.org/

Ask Jefferson Web Site:
http://etext.virginia.edu/jefferson/quotations

Jefferson's Home at Monticello:
http://www.monticello.org

Library of Congress Web Site "Temple of Liberty, Building
a Capitol":
http://www.loc.gov/exhibits/us.capitol/s0.html

Eyewitness to History—Hamilton–Burr Duel:
http://www.eyewitnesstohistory.com/duel.htm

Presidential Elections Results:
http://www.multied.com/elections

Presidential Biographies:
http://www.whitehouse.gov/history/presidents/
http://www.presidentsusa.net/bio.html

Erie Canal Home Page:
http://www.eriecanal.org/

Historic Atlas Resource:
http://mappinghistory.uoregon.edu/english/US/us.html

Lewis and Clark Expedition:
http://www.lewisclark.net/

Native Americans on The Trail of Tears:
http://www.crystalinks.com/trailoftears.html

Library of Congress—Time Line Page:
http://lcweb2.loc.gov/ammem/vfwhtml/vfwtl.html

History of the War of 1812:
http://www.multied.com/1812/

Battle of New Orleans:
http://www.eyewitnesstohistory.com/battleofneworleans.htm

Mexican War:
http://www.dmwv.org/mexwar/history/concise.htm

Chapter Six

Causes of the Civil War:
http://americancivilwar.com/kids_zone/causes.html

U.S. Census Bureau:
http://www.census.gov

Amistad Slave Mutiny—Famous Trials:
http://www.law.umkc.edu/faculty/projects/ftrials/amistad/
AMISTD.HTM

Uncle Tom's Cabin:
http://etext.lib.virginia.edu/toc/modeng/public/StoCabi.html

Abraham Lincoln Biography:
http://www.whitehouse.gov/history/presidents/al16.html

Lincoln Resources—Internet Public Library POTUS
(Presidents of the United States):
http://www.ipl.org/div/potus/alincoln.html

Outline of the Civil War:
http://www.greatamericanhistory.net/outlines.htm

Library of Congress—Matthew Brady:
http://memory.loc.gov/ammem/cwphtml/cwphome.html

National Archives—Emancipation Proclamation:
http://www.archives.gov/exhibits/featured_documents/
emancipation_proclamation/

Formal Portraits of Ulysses S. Grant and Robert E. Lee:
http://memory.loc.gov/ammem/cwphtml/

Lincoln Assassination Page:
http://lcwe62.loc.gov/ammem/alhtml/alrintr.html

Ford's Theatre:
http://www.fordstheatre.org/

Andrew Johnson Impeachment:
http://www.impeach-andrewjohnson.com/

Chapter Seven

Ulysses S. Grant Home Page:
http://www.empirenet.com/~ulysses/

Age of Industry:
http://www.wcisel.com/curric98/industrial_revolution_
inventors.htm

Public Broadcasting System's American Experience Program
on Carnegie:
http://www.pbs.org/wgbh/pages/amex/carnegie/

Carnegie Corporation of New York Kids Page:
http://www.carnegie.org/sub/kids/index.html

John D. Rockefeller:
http://www.micheloud.com/FXM/SO/jdr.htm

Newport Mansions:
http://www.NewportMansions.org/

Labor History Time Line:
http://www.iam2208.org/labor_history.htm

Biography of Samuel Gompers:
http://www.kentlaw.edu/ilhs/gompers.htm

PBS Make Your Own Family Tree:
http://pbskids.org/wayback/family/tree/index.html

History Channel Spotlight on Ellis Island:
http://www.historychannel.com/ellisisland/index2.html

Ellis Island:
http://www.ellisisland.org

George A. Custer and the Battle of Little Big Horn:
http://www.pbs.org/weta/thewest/resources/archives/six/
bighorn.htm

Eyewitness Account Custer's Last Stand:
http://www.eyewitnesstohistory.com/custer.htm

Chapter Eight

World's Columbian Exhibition:
http://xroads.virginia.edu/~MA96/WCE/title.html

"In the Depths of a Coal Mine" by Stephen Crane:
http://ehistory.osu.edu/osu/mmh/gildedage/content/
CraneDepths.cfm

Sagamore Hill:
http://www.theodore-roosevelt.com/trsahi.html

Biographies of Progressive Presidents:
http://www.ipl.org/div/potus/

The Sinking of the *Maine*:
http://www.smplanet.com/imperialism/remember.html

The Splendid Little War:
http://www.smplanet.com/imperialism/splendid.html

New York Public Library—The 100th Anniversary of the
Spanish-American War:
http://www.nypl.org/research/chss/epo/spanexhib/index.html

1898–1998 Centennial of the Spanish American War:
http://www.zpub.com/cpp/saw.html

Public Broadcasting System's The Great War:
http://www.pbs.org/greatwar/timeline/

Trenches on the Web:
http://www.worldwar1.com/

Roaring 20s:
http://www.1920-30.com/

Biographies of Harding, Coolidge, and Hoover:
http://www.ipl.org/div/potus/

Biography of Henry Ford:
http://www.thehenryford.org/exhibits/hf/

Library of Congress Exhibit—Votes for Women 1850–1920:
http://lcweb2.loc.gov/ammem/vfwhtml/vfwhome.html

Women Win the Right to Vote—Biographies of Influential
Suffragists:
http://www.rochester.edu/SBA/suffragebios.html

Flapper Culture and Style Page:
http://faculty.pittstate.edu/~knichols/jazzage.html#flapper

Ohio State's American Temperance and Prohibition Page:
http://prohibition.osu.edu/

Famous Trials of the Twentieth Century Scopes:
http://www.law.umkc.edu/faculty/projects/ftrials/scopes/
scopes.htm

Famous Trials of the Twentieth Century Sacco-Vanzetti:
http://www.law.umkc.edu/faculty/projects/ftrials/SaccoV/
SaccoV.htm

Chapter Nine

Herbert Hoover Presidential Library at the National
Archives:
http://hoover.nara.gov/

Fireside Chat:
http://www.mhrcc.org/fdr/chat1.html

The Federal Writers Project from the Library of Congress:
http://rs6.loc.gov/ammem/wpaintro/exhome.html

Dust Bowl From the Library of Congress Voices from the Dust Bowl:
http://lcweb2.loc.gov/ammem/afctshtml/tshome.html

Public Broadcasting System's American Experience Surviving the Dust Bowl:
http://www.pbs.org/wgbh/pages/amex/dustbowl/

Michigan Historical Society's Great Depression Gallery:
http://www.sos.state.mi.us/history/museum/explore/museums/hismus/1900-75/depressn/index.html

On-line History of World War II:
http://www.historyplace.com/

Radio Days—News:
http://www.otr.com/news.html

Pearl Harbor Remembered Exhibit:
http://my.execpc.com/~dschaaf/mainmenu.html

Library of Congress' Exhibit: Women on the Front:
http://lcweb.loc.gov/exhibits/wcf/wcf0001.html

Wartime Posters from the National Archives:
http://www.archives.gov/exhibits/powers_of_persuasion/man_the_guns/man_the_guns.html

Japanese-American Internment:
http://www.archives.gov/research/alic/reference/military/japanese-internment.html

Holocaust Museum:
http://www.ushmm.org/

World War II History:
http://www.multied.com/ww2/index.html

D-Day Memorial:
http://www.dday.org

The Manhattan Project:
http://www.cfo.doe.gov/me70/manhattan/index.htm

Hiroshima Archive:
http://www.lclark.edu/~history/HIROSHIMA/

The Franklin D. Roosevelt Museum:
http://www.fdrlibrary.marist.edu/

FDR Memorial:
http://www.nps.gov/fdrm/home.htm

Chapter Ten

United Nations:
http://www.un.org

Cold War Hot Links Page:
http://homepages.stmartin.edu/fac_staff/dprice/cold.war.htm

Cold War Policies Page:
http://history.sandiego.edu/gen/20th/coldwar0.html

Politics and Social Attitudes of the Cold War Page:
http://library.thinkquest.org/3266/

Library of Congress 50th Anniversary of the Marshall Plan:
http://rs7.loc.gov/exhibits/marshall/mars0.html

The U.S. Air Force's Berlin Airlift Web Site:
http://www.af.mil/historysearchBerlinAirlift

The United States NATO Mission Page:
http://nato.usmission.gov/

Examining the Korean War:
http://mcel.pacificu.edu/as/students/stanley/home.html

The Korean War Veterans Memorial:
http://www.nab.usace.army.mil/projects/WashingtonDC/
korean.html

Truman Presidential Library Site:
http://www.trumanlibrary.org/

Eisenhower and the Cold War:
http://countrystudies.us/united-states/history-112.htm

McCarthy—The Multi-Media Web Site:
http://www.americanrhetoric.com/speeches/welch-mccarthy.html

Rosenberg Famous Trial Page:
http://www.law.umkc.edu/faculty/projects/ftrials/rosenb/ROSENB.HTM

Literature and Culture of the American 1950s:
http://www.writing.upenn.edu/~afilreis/50s/home.html

Unofficial Elvis Presley Home Page:
http://sunsite.unc.edu/elvis/elvishom.html

History of TV:
http://www.tvhistory.tv/

Black History Links:
http://www.suelebeau.com/blackhistory.htm

Breaking the Color Line:
http://lcweb2.loc.gov/ammem/jrhtml/jrabout.html

National Archives—Jackie Robinson:
http://www.suelebeau.com/blackhistory.htm 227

Brown v. Board of Education Exhibit:
http://www.cjonline.com/indepth/brown/

National Civil Rights Museum:
http://www.civilrightsmuseum.org/

Eisenhower Presidential Library:
http://www.eisenhower.archives.gov/

National Aeronautics and Space Administration's (NASA)
U.S. Human Space Flight Site:
http://spaceflight.nasa.gov/home/index.html

Cuban Missile Crisis Aerial Photo Page:
http://www.fas.org/irp/imint/cuba.htm

The 14 Days in October Site:
http://library.thinkquest.org/11046/

Berlin Wall:
http://www.dailysoft.com/berlinwall/index.html

The Kennedy Assassination:
http://mcadams.posc.mu.edu/home.htm

John F. Kennedy Library:
http://www.jfklibrary.org/

Martin Luther King I Have a Dream Speech:
http://www.americanrhetoric.com/speeches/
mlkihaveadream.htm

Public Broadcasting System's Point of View—Dissect an Ad:
http://www.pbs.org/pov/ad/index.html

Lyndon Johnson Presidential Library:
http://www.lbjlib.utexas.edu/

Vietnam War History Page:
http://www.digitalhistory.uh.edu/modules/vietnam/index.cfm

Gulf of Tonkin Resolution:
http://www.fair.org/media-beat/940727.html

Chapter Eleven

Martin Luther King Project:
http://www.leland.stanford.edu/group/King/

Robert F. Kennedy Assassination:
http://homepages.tcp.co.uk/~dlewis/

Robert F. Kennedy Memorial:
http://www.rfkmemorial.org/

Famous American Trials—Chicago 7:
http://www.law.umkc.edu/faculty/projects/ftrials/Chicago7/
chicago7.html

Kent State Memorial:
http://www.library.kent.edu/page/13950

The National Archives Exhibit Nixon and Watergate:
http://www.archives.gov/exhibits/american_originals/
nixon.html

The Washington Post's Interactive Watergate Site:
http://www.washingtonpost.com/wp-srv/politics/special/
watergate/index.html

Watergate Decade:
http://www.journale.com/watergate.html

Northwestern University Supreme Court Oyez Site:
http://oyez.org

Vietnam Vets Vietnam Veterans Memorial:
http://www.vietvet.org/thewall.htm

Gerald Ford Presidential Library:
http://www.ford.utexas.edu/

Jimmy Carter Presidential Library:
http://www.jimmycarterlibrary.org/

Jimmy Carter Center:
http://www.cartercenter.org/homepage.html

Challenger Accident Web Site:
http://www.fas.org/spp/51L.html

PBS—Iran-Contra Affair:
http://www.pbs.org/wgbh/amex/reagan/peopleevents/
pande08.html

Ronald Reagan Presidential Library:
http://www.reaganlibrary.com/

George H. W. Bush Presidential Library:
http://bushlibrary.tamu.edu/

Operation Desert Storm:
http://www.historycentral.com/desert_storm/index.html

William Jefferson Clinton 1993 Inauguration:
http://clinton4.nara.gov/WH/Family/html/inauguration
1993.html

1993 World Trade Center Bombing:
http://www.milnet.com/milnet/wtc.htm

Oklahoma Federal Building Explosion Museum:
http://www.oklahomacitynationalmemorial.org/

Frontline: Waco, the Inside Story:
http://www.pbs.org/wgbh/pages/frontline/waco/

Famous Trials Bill Clinton Impeachment:
http://www.law.umkc.edu/faculty/projects/ftrials/clinton/
clintonhome.html

Chapter Twelve

The 2000 Election:
http://www.historycentral.com/elections/2000.html

2000 Election Map:
http://www.historycentral.com/elections/2000map.html

Election Recount Chronology:
http://www.historycentral.com/elections/2000recount.html

Popular vote Pie Chart:
http://www.historycentral.com/elections/2000pop.html

Bush vs. Gore:
http://encyclopedia.kids.net.au/page/bu/Bush_v._Gore

George W. Bush Inauguration:
http://www.cnn.com/ALLPOLITICS/inauguration/2001/

Library of Congress:
http://memory.loc.gov/ammem/collections/911_archive/

September 11, 2001:
http://www.september11news.com/

American Museum of American History 9/11 Exhibit:
http://americanhistory.si.edu/september11/collection/
index.asp

Pentagon Memorial Site:
http://memorial.pentagon.mil/

World Trade Center Memorial:
http://www.national911memorial.org/site/
PageServer?pagename=homepage2

Flight 92 Memorial:
http://www.nps.gov/flni

Operation Enduring Freedom:
http://www.historycentral.com/enduringfreedom/index.html

Operation Iraqi Freedom:
http://www.pbs.org/wgbh/pages/frontline/shows/invasion/

Interactive Iraq: Five Years at War:
http://www.cbsnews.com/elements/2008/03/12/iraq/
interactivehomemenu3930959.shtml

California Recall:
http://www.washingtonpost.com/wp-dyn/politics/specials/
califrecall/

Space Shuttle Columbia NASA tribute (2003):
http://www.nasa.gov/columbia/home/index.html

Race for the White House 2004:
http://www.gwu.edu/~action/P2004.html

Hurricane Katrina:
http://www.katrinadestruction.com/

Biography of Chief Justice Rogerts:
http://www.oyez.org/justices/john_g_roberts_jr/

Tour of Supreme Court:
http://www.oyez.org/tour/

Nancy Pelosi Kids Page:
http://speaker.house.gov/kids/

Election 2008:
http://www.timeforkids.com/TFK/election08/
http://www.weeklyreader.com/election/index.asp

INDEX

NOTES

NOTES